Governing's Guide to Performance Measurement for Geniuses (and Other Public Managers)

JONATHAN WALTERS

GOVERNING MANAGEMENT SERIES

Governing Books, Washington, D.C.

Published by GOVERNING Books
A division of GOVERNING Magazine
1100 Connecticut Ave. N.W., Suite 1300
Washington, DC 20036
www.governing.com

Printed in the United States of America

Book design: Richard Steadham
Cover and inside illustrations: David Clark

Library of Congress Cataloging-in-Publication Data

Walters, Jonathan, 1955-
   Measuring up : governing's guide to performance measurement for
geniuses (and other public managers) / Jonathan Walters
      p.   cm.
   Includes bibliographical references and index.
   ISBN 1-56802-458-4 (pbk. : alk. paper)
      1. Government productivity—United States—Measurement.
   2. Administrative agencies—United States—Evaluation. 3. State
governments—United States—Evaluation. 4. Local government—United
States—Evaluation. I. Title.
   JK2445.P76W33 1998
   352.3'0973—dc21   98-40498
                                                                CIP

FIRST EDITION
THIRD PRINTING

To Ma

Contents

Thanks

First, a huge thanks to those who agreed to read the manuscript of this book, among whom are also people who have spent tons of time teaching me (or trying to teach me, anyway) about performance measurement in government.

They include Harry Hatry at the Urban Institute; Marv Weidner and Mary Reavely in Iowa; Dick Tracy in Portland, Oregon; Marcia Calicchia from Cornell University; Shelley Metzenbaum, formerly with the U.S. EPA, now director of the Performance Measurement Project at the Kennedy School of Government, who was working on her own tome on performance measurement when I asked her to read mine; the journalism team of Katherine Barrett and Richard Greene, who, thankfully, didn't pull any punches in their evaluation of the book; and Jeffrey Tryens, executive director of the Oregon Progress Board, who—speaking of not pulling any punches—called the book "nauseatingly flip" (he's still a great guy). Special thanks to Martha Marshall in Prince William County, Virginia, who has a great sense of humor about all this stuff and who has also taught me something about persistence, and to Jay Fountain at the Governmental Accounting Standards Board, who has probably spent more time on the phone with me than he has with any member of his own family—his detailed critique was invaluable, and he hung in there even in the face of the dumbest questions I could throw at him.

Thanks also to my mom, Kate, and my sister, Sue, who both read the book and who both laughed out loud while reading it (I think for the right reasons). And thanks also to Lizzie Ehrenhalt, who in the midst of taking driver's ed classes still offered to help me do Internet research.

But the book never would have happened without the help and support of three people in particular: my editor (and co-conspirator), John Martin, who egged me on the whole way; the book's designer, Richard Steadham, who has enough to do without taking on more work like this; and above all GOVERNING's publisher, Peter Harkness, who is a ton of fun to work with, in part because he doesn't mind throwing the occasional Hail Mary pass.

Finally, thanks to Eileen, who brought me good (non-alcoholic) mixed drinks while I typed and good (alcoholic) mixed drinks when I was done typing.

Thanks to you all.

Jonathan Walters
Ghent, New York

3

Performance Measurement and Why Bob Got Thrown Out of the House

Consider, just for the fun of it, an off-the-top-of-the-head list of the management trends and trendlettes that public officials have had to contend with since the beginning of the Reinventing Government wave: Total Quality Management, benchmarking, reengineering, value engineering, earned-value performance, rightsizing, working to core mission, downsizing, flattening, privatizing, integrated systems management, the Balanced Scorecard, strategic visioning...blah, blah, blah.

Confusion mixed with exasperation is, understandably, the operative reaction. So the rightly wary public manager would do well to ask what is so special about performance measurement—what distinguishes it from the other quick fixits they've been subjected to over the course of their careers?

Well, most bluntly put, unlike all those other trends that reared up and then disappeared without so much as a ripple, it looks like performance measurement is here to stay, at least for while.

Now, that may not be the most compelling argument for why performance measurement is worth a look. So let's pull a page out of the politician's "How to Talk Down to Citizens" handbook to try to lay a more solid foundation under the justification for learning more about performance measurement.

One of the basic techniques used in that handbook is to reduce public policy and public administration to household analogy. The most popular of these household analogies, of course, has been the one used to argue in favor of a bal-

4

anced-budget amendment to the United States Constitution. You've heard it: "Bob and Mary Smith have to balance their household budget, so the federal government should have to, too." Never mind that Bob and Mary Smith are in debt up to their Jockey shorts thanks to credit cards, the car payment, the mortgage, Bob Sr.'s compulsive gambling habit and Bob Jr.'s insistence on getting his art history degree from the most expensive college in the country.

Which is to say that these analogies are invariably incredibly simplistic and pretty condescending, to boot. But they can be useful, in a crude sort of way, to drive home a point that otherwise might get lost in the explaining. So here we apply it to making the case in favor of performance measurement in government.

Were a politician to extend the household analogy to performance measurement in government, it would go something like this: Bob and Mary Smith are newly married and living on a very tight budget. Bob comes home from the local mall one evening and announces to Mary that he's just spent 211.55 of the household's precious dollars while wandering through the mall's many and dazzling shops. Mary is naturally curious about what Bob got for that $211.55 and how that spending contributes to the present and future well-being of the household. So Mary asks Bob in greater detail about his adventure.

While Bob is able to produce a concrete list of the goodies he procured—cigars, a new putter and two cans of his favorite spiced peanuts—he's at a total loss when it comes to explaining how any of them contribute to the ultimate well-being of the household enterprise. Put into the jargon of performance measurement, Bob can define for Mary the "inputs" involved in his adventure: His time, plus the $211.55. (If you're a real stickler, you can also figure in gas; wear and tear on the car; insurance for the car amortized over the length of the ride to and from the mall; the cost of his health insurance likewise amortized, since any trip to the mall is likely to induce either insanity or injury or both;

and so forth.) Bob can describe the "activity" pretty easily, too: driving to the mall and dropping a bundle of dough. And, finally, he can define the "outputs" of the trip: good cigars, a very nice putter (the performance of which has yet to be judged) and a couple of cans of his favorite snack food.

But where Bob gets in some serious trouble is in the critical area of "outcomes." The vision statement that Bob and Mary agreed on when they got married was: "To work together to ensure the security and happiness of the household unit." One specific "goal" related to that vision was: "To set aside enough money for a down payment on a suburban tract home with wall-to-wall carpeting and a finished basement." There is, unfortunately for Bob, no specific goal under their vision statement that involves stinking up the house with cigar smoke, lowering his handicap or getting fat. Mary throws Bob out of the house.

Well, that is a gross simplification of the whole performance measurement concept (and condescending, too). But it captures the essence of why performance measurement has become the driving trend in federal, state and local government administration today: Citizens want to know what's being accomplished with their tax dollars, not just how much is being spent and on what. Which is why a growing number of government officials—particularly elected government officials—are starting to ask the same thing. (Although, as we'll learn later in this book, enthusiasm for performance measurement among some elected officials can wane a tad once it occurs to them that performance measurement might be used to hold *them* accountable for some results, too.)

This basic message—that citizens want government to deliver quality services that yield good results (and do it without raising taxes)—arrives at a time when life for public officials is getting more, not less, complicated.

And so the times increasingly have called for an approach to public administration that, to be direct about it, focuses on deliverables. A growing number of experts now argue that an indispensable component of meeting that call for greater accountability is a much more accurate assessment of what outcomes the public is getting for its tax dollars, whether those outcomes involve tasty drinking water, smarter kids, welfare recipients being shepherded to self-sufficiency or a safer world.

Some Good (and Bad) Reasons for Pursuing Performance Measurement

The fact that citizens are getting testy about insisting on a bottom-line look at what government is producing is one very good reason for pursuing performance measurement. That, in turn, is why an increasing number of jurisdictions are publishing basic "report cards" on their own performance. But another persuasive reason why performance measurement is worth a second look is that the practice either is, or soon will be, mandatory for all levels of government.

At the federal level, the Government Performance and Results Act—known Washington-wide as either "GPRA" (pronounced "jipra") or simply "the Results Act"—mandates that all federal departments start measuring results. Meanwhile, the Governmental Accounting Standards Board—the High Ministry of governmental accounting rules for state and local governments—will within the next few years probably begin asking all states and localities to start reporting "service efforts and accomplishments"—accountant jargon for "activities" and "results," or simply performance measurement.

But there are important reasons for pursuing performance measurement other than that you're soon going to have to, or that politicians and citizens will be demanding it. In fact, from a pure public administration standpoint, those are probably the least important reasons for doing performance measurement.

The most important reason is that in doing performance measurement, public officials can begin to tinker with (or overhaul) the process between collecting tax dollars and achieving some public goal with some confidence that government will be able to calculate the tinkering's impact by gauging changes in results.

Some have argued that there is one other major reason why performance measurement is worth trying. They say that by making fiscal decisions more of a science (by tying budgets directly to concrete results), those fiscal decisions will become less political and more outcomes-based.

The idea that performance measurement will take the politics out of budgeting—or out of governing, generally—is the least plausible of all the claims made for it. But certainly, if done in a realistic and sophisticated way, performance measurement does offer public officials and outside observers a powerful tool for analyzing some of the real impacts of governmental spending and subsequent program activity. In hand, such information could, indeed, begin to better inform debates over resource allocation.

But even if the connection between outcomes and budgets stays fuzzy, there is one other area in which a focus on results can have a profound impact, and that is on how a particular program or service is managed. Once an office or department starts to focus on results, there tends to follow an attendant hard look at whether the shop is really operating in a way that focuses resources in an intelligent, efficient way on achieving those results. The U.S. Department of Veterans Affairs, for example, has won widespread and well-deserved praise for improvements in the whole range of services and care that it provides for veterans, improvements that have flowed directly from the department's relatively new focus on results.

When applied intelligently, in other words, performance measurement really does hold out the potential for improving how government runs.

A Concise History of Performance Measurement in Government

Performance measurement is not a new idea. When legendary New York City wonder-Mayor Fiorello LaGuardia was looking for a public health director back in the 1930s, he didn't put together any politically inclusive, borough-balanced, race- and gender-representative search committee of New York big thinkers, movers and shakers. Nor did he go the in-law route, which wasn't his style anyway. He didn't even offer the job to some major political patron, which wasn't his style either (at least until his later administrations).

Rather, he gathered up public health statistics from major cities around the country, and then he went after the guy with the best numbers. Period.

Since then, public managers have been subjected to a wide and incessant variety of results-based management reforms, including such impressive-sounding exercises as Management by Objectives and Program Planning Budgeting.

The results of those management trends haven't always been better results. But it can be argued that each of those trends moved government another inexorable step closer to its current fascination with the bottom line: performance measurement.

End of history. For more thorough coverage of the history of performance measurement in the federal government, read pages 93 and 94 of *Inside the Reinvention Machine*, published by the Brookings Institution and edited by Donald F. Kettl and John J. DiIulio Jr.

The Dangers of Performance Measurement

But for all its potential, there is a huge caveat that must be emphasized when it comes to performance measurement: There is real danger in losing perspective, both in the implementation of performance measurement and in using whatever data ends up standing in for "performance."

A mindless preoccupation with the process of implementing performance measurement is grossly counterproductive. A department can get itself turned sideways and then backwards in flow charts and multiple meetings, with the ultimate goal of efficiency and effectiveness disappearing into that murky quagmire called process.

A mindless focus on data can, likewise, have a perverse effect. Allowing mere numbers to drive programs and budgets can be a dangerous game. If all a city council looks at when judging a police department's performance is crime statistics, then the police are going to quickly arrive at the conclusion that the best approach to crime fighting is to invoke an 8 p.m.-to-6 a.m curfew for everybody citywide. If a state economic development office is judged only by the number of businesses it lures to the state every year, then that office is going to lobby the legislature to eliminate all environmental, health and safety, fraud, and consumer protection legislation and argue for a 50-year tax moratorium on all newcomers. And if a key measure of a municipal fire company's effectiveness is response times, then that fire company is going to vigorously argue against things like narrow, winding streets, on-street parking, speed bumps and other "traffic calmers" that many communities have found actually enhance livability (and housing values), even as they occasionally (or even chronically) compromise public safety.

In other words, applying performance measurement to what government does is not a math equation. It is a complicated and frequently very messy art. Using isolated performance measures as any sort of ultimate driver of governmental decision-making is dumb. "Results" always have to be judged in the broader context of the greater good.

A Public Official's Handy Pocket Primer on Performance Measurement

1. If performance measurement sounds a lot like common sense, that's because it *is* common sense.

2. If performance measurement feels like a drill you've been through before, that's because you *have* been through it before, one way or another. The difference this time around is that some of these people actually seem to know what they're talking about; what's more, they're serious.

3. Performance measurement is no quick fix. If your agency director drags you all into the main hall of the Senator Hank P. Gasbag State Office Building and announces that the agency will be transformed within the next six months on account of performance measures, it's time to either take that early buyout the governor's been dangling in front of you or find a nice, secluded corner of your office building and hide there until this all blows over.

4. Ignore No. 3. Waiting performance measurement out as just another management fad may not, actually, be a viable strategy. It's looking like the Governmental Accounting Standards Board—the gang in Norwalk, Connecticut, that sets accounting standards for state and local government—will be making it mandatory in the next few years. For you feds, the jig is already up. Congress already requires you do it by way of the Government Performance and Results Act.

5. Find a good book on performance measurement and start figuring out how to make it work for you and your program.

CHAPTER ONE

Sick of Being a Basket Case

Being a cop in Long Beach, California, in the late 1980s wasn't much fun. It wasn't much fun in large part because in that great fight between good and evil, evil was putting up some impressive numbers: Between 1983 and 1990, crime in Long Beach increased by 30 percent; violent crime doubled. In fact, being a Long Beach cop was so little fun that the department was having trouble keeping people on the job; it couldn't even fill all of its budgeted staff positions. After all, how many fresh young faces are going to show up downtown based on a recruitment ad that reads: "Lousy pay! Lousy hours! The regular threat of physical harm! Join a losing team today!"

But if the police were having a tough time, think of what it was like to be a city council member. A soaring violent crime rate doesn't do much for one's standing in the polls.

The public and the press, meanwhile, were as sympathetic as ever, which is to say, they took every opportunity to kick the stuffing out of both the police department and the city council.

Clearly, something had to be done, and what had to be done in some city council members' minds was obvious: get rid of the police department altogether. The way to do that was through a tactic being employed by lots of governments in a wide variety of policy and program areas: contract the job out, in this case to the Los Angeles County sheriff's department. (The sports equivalent of that thinking: Have Montreal disband the Expos and then contract out their standing in the National League East to the Florida Marlins.)

But while shedding all accountability for the performance of a police department had obvious bottom-line political appeal, when it came to the critical vote on whether to actually do that, five of the nine city council members bravely chose instead to fix the department they had. The basic tool to which they turned in order to accomplish that was an even more recent public administration fad than contracting out: performance measurement. And so Long Beach put together a team of officials to refocus the police on something new and exciting: results.

Shifting Focus: From Response to Results

The Long Beach police department, while in poor shape in the early 1990s, shouldn't be singled out here for criticism. Before this particular performance measurement wave (it is by no means the first, but this one has some serious legs; see "A Concise History of Performance Measurement in Government" on page 9), an amazingly large number of police departments nationwide had for years been approaching their jobs in a less than logical fashion: They weren't focused on results, they were focused on response. In fact, members of the Long Beach PD had the distinct impression that they were spending a good portion of their time running around like chickens with their heads turned around backwards, racing from one call to another, never getting out of their cars except to deal with problems, and often returning to the same scene over and over to solve—or, to be painfully accurate about it, not solve—the same problem again and again. Sometimes they didn't answer calls at all.

In the meantime, they were having very few positive experiences with the community they were sworn to protect. In return—as one might expect—they were getting very little help and support from the community they were sworn to protect. The bottom line was that the department just wasn't solving—or preventing—very many crimes.

Now, if this were a book written by a management consultant, this would be the part where we would include the flow chart mapping out the intricate process by which Long Beach reinvented its police department (see the next page for an example of the genre). That flow chart would look something like an hour's worth of flight patterns around O'Hare Airport, one of the more complicated offensive plays of the Green Bay Packers, or the midnight ramblings of a stray dog on his regular trash-can run.

Better to handle it by saying that the first thing the police department did was to start where it should have started: with the citizens of Long Beach. Step one was to survey Long Beach residents on their attitudes about safety, crime and the police. The city chose this route based on that hard-to-dispute theory of public administration that when it comes to performance, how citizens feel about both government, generally, and what government is accomplishing, specifically, is a thing of some consequence. But the rationale for polling citizens was based on another radical notion that was sweeping public administration at the time: that citizens are "customers" of government and that satisfied customers are the goal of good government.

Now, if this were an academic book, the next 17 billion words—half a chapter, roughly—would be devoted to a debate over the definition of "customer," and whether government can even have "customers," and aren't taxpayers

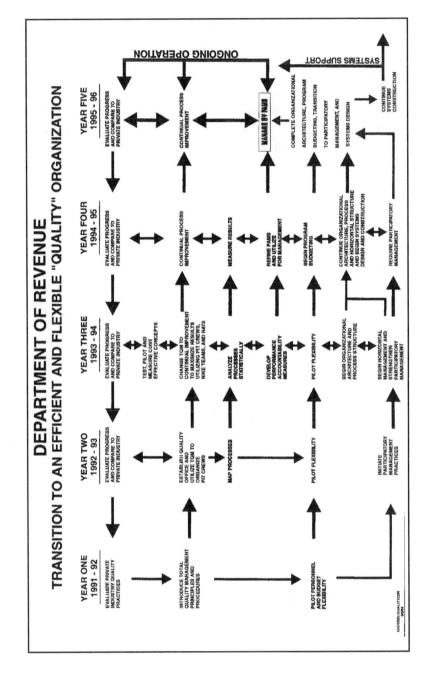

DEPARTMENT OF REVENUE
TRANSITION TO AN EFFICIENT AND FLEXIBLE "QUALITY" ORGANIZATION

ONGOING OPERATION

SYSTEMS SUPPORT

YEAR ONE
1991 - 92

EVALUATE PRIVATE INDUSTRY QUALITY PRACTICES

INTRODUCE TOTAL QUALITY MANAGEMENT PRINCIPLES AND PROCEDURES

PILOT PERSONNEL AND BUDGET FLEXIBILITY

YEAR TWO
1992 - 93

EVALUATE PROGRESS AND COMPARE TO PRIVATE INDUSTRY

ESTABLISH QUALITY OFFICE AND UTILIZE TQM TO ORGANIZE PIT CREWS

MAP PROCESSES

PILOT FLEXIBILITY

INITIATE PARTICIPATORY MANAGEMENT PRACTICES

YEAR THREE
1993 - 94

EVALUATE PROGRESS AND COMPARE TO PRIVATE INDUSTRY

TEST, PILOT AND MEASURE COST EFFECTIVE CONCEPTS

CHANGE TQM TO CONTINUAL IMPROVEMENT TO MAXIMIZE RESULTS UTILIZING PIT CREWS, NIKE TEAMS, AND RATS

ANALYZE PROCESSES STATISTICALLY

DEVELOP PERFORMANCE ACCOUNTABILITY MEASURES

PILOT FLEXIBILITY

BEGIN ORGANIZATIONAL ARCHITECTURE AND PROCESS STRUCTURE

BEGIN HORIZONTAL MANAGEMENT AND STRENGTHEN PARTICIPATORY MANAGEMENT

YEAR FOUR
1994 - 95

EVALUATE PROGRESS AND COMPARE TO PRIVATE INDUSTRY

CONTINUAL PROCESS IMPROVEMENT

MEASURE RESULTS

REFINE PAMS AND UTILIZE FOR MANAGEMENT

BEGIN PROGRAM BUDGETING

CONTINUE ORGANIZATIONAL ARCHITECTURE, PROCESS AND HORIZONTAL STRUCTURE DESIGN AND CONSTRUCTION

REQUIRE PARTICIPATORY MANAGEMENT

YEAR FIVE
1995 - 96

EVALUATE PROGRESS AND COMPARE TO PRIVATE INDUSTRY

CONTINUAL PROCESS IMPROVEMENT

MANAGE BY PAMS

COMPLETE ORGANIZATIONAL ARCHITECTURE, PROGRAM BUDGETING, TRANSITION TO PARTICIPATORY MANAGEMENT, AND SYSTEMS DESIGN

CONTINUE SYSTEMS CONSTRUCTION

CHCORE3/QUALITY.CDR 8/94

16

really "owners," and so forth. We'll forgo all that and note that citizens do rely on government for—in fact do pay government for—certain services and products, and that government's end of the bargain is to deliver those services and products...and perhaps even some meaningful results. One can describe that relationship any way one wants and in as many words as one would like. But the more successful governments and government agencies in the country, such as Phoenix or Virginia or the U.S. Department of Veterans Affairs, call those people who need or expect service from government "customers." The connection is pretty clear, argue those who are comfortable with the word. Once governmental entities start viewing those it serves as customers, organizational behavior tends to change in positive ways. (For a brief discussion of "customer," including an inadequate explanation of "inside" versus "outside" customer, see "A Government Official's Guide to Customers" at the end of this chapter).

Bad Numbers, Bad News

Anyway, Long Beach went to its citizen/customers to ask how they felt about local law enforcement. What the city found was predictable: Residents of Long Beach didn't think much of their boys and girls in blue. Fewer than half the residents polled, for example, thought the department was "community oriented." Nor did residents think much of their chances of making it through the year without getting mugged. Half the residents polled said they didn't feel safe in their own neighborhoods.

That got a lot of people's attention, and it led to a series of public meetings. The subject of those meetings was, again, straightforward: what it was that citizens didn't like about the department and its performance; what citizens wanted from their police department; and how citizens and police could begin working more closely together to make

Long Beach a safe place in which to live and do business.

The department, very wisely, didn't just talk to citizens, though. It also polled its own staff, many of whom were as frustrated as Long Beach residents were over the department's performance. And so the LBPD asked its own employees about work conditions, the quality of equipment, pay, the attitude of upper management toward the grunts, and so forth. Not very surprisingly, the results there weren't glowing, either.

In trying to get a handle on the poor performance of its police department, the city took two other steps: First, it analyzed future trends—demographic to economic—that might impact the rise and fall of crime in the city. That allowed police officials to plan even more strategically as they looked at new ways to run their department. But LBPD officials did one other thing, a thing that is never very popular: They compared Long Beach's police force and its performance with those of 10 other departments around the state. What they found, says performance measurement expert Scott Bryant, who was working as an internal consultant with the city at the time, was that the Long Beach PD tended to rank high—high, that is, in the cost of providing police services and rates of violent crime.

The picture that emerged from all this was predictably bleak: By just about any measure, the LBPD was doing a lousy job. The citizens of Long Beach didn't trust or like the department very much. Morale in the department was in the tank. And "We May Be Expensive, but at Least We're Ineffective" wasn't a new slogan that many people were going to rally around.

Turning it Around

Having gathered lots of depressing information about crime, law enforcement, police/community relations and internal police department attitudes in its fair city, the Long

Beach PD took what in some circles is considered a controversial next step: It came up with a "vision statement."

The step is considered controversial because there are those who believe that this whole business of vision statements is a bunch of touchy-feely nonsense. After all, what a police department is supposed to be doing is pretty obvious. What a state environmental protection agency is supposed to be doing is pretty obvious. What the U.S. Social Security Administration is supposed to be doing is pretty obvious. Do they really need vision statements to guide them in their work? The empiricists among us—those who've been watching governmental organizations wrestle with change and progress for a while—invariably shrug and say: "Well, it may sound silly, but it really seems to help."

The fact is, even the most maudlin, banal, redundant, elementary vision statement serves an important purpose: It helps build consensus around what an organization ought to be doing, and it focuses people on the tasks at hand. And in a large organization with a complicated or tough job, that isn't such a bad thing. To wit, the Long Beach police department's vision statement:

People in Long Beach will:
- *Feel Safe in the Community*
- *Work Together to Solve Community and Neighborhood Problems*
- *Have a High Level of Respect, Trust and Confidence in Their Police Department*

Again, these all seem obvious. But having them down on paper does seem to get everybody looking in the same direction.

With the vision set, the city then developed a more specific set of goals flowing from the vision statement aimed at moving the department in the right direction. In all, the city came up with 14 specific goals in four broad categories all aimed at meeting the three-part vision statement (see "The Long Beach P.D.'s 14-Step Plan for Kicking the Losing Habit" at the end of this chapter).

CHAPTER ONE

From Strategy to the Street

OK, the tricky part about all of this, and the point at which real performance measures come into play: You've got agreement on a vision; you've got consensus on narrower goals that flow from the vision statement. How do you know if you're making progress toward them? How can you be sure that whatever action you're taking, whatever resources you're expending, whatever new tactics you're employing are actually getting you the results you're after? The answer: performance measures, which are also known in the business as "performance indicators." In the case of Long Beach, they were referred to as "measures of success."

Long Beach came up with 100 of them. They ranged from such basics as the number of gang-related crimes committed over a certain time period, to response times to various kinds of calls, to cases cleared. Pretty straightforward. But the department also started measuring some other areas, areas that some argue are even more relevant to the performance of a law enforcement agency than nailing crooks. Using citizen surveys, the department started asking Long Beach-ites how safe they felt from day to day and how they would rate the police department as an outfit that was approachable and responsive. The idea, of course, was to get baseline data in these key areas so that progress, or lack of it, could then be tracked as the department tried its new, more results-based approach to policing.

In Long Beach—and in theory—all the pieces were supposed to line up something like this:

• Vision: That citizens will "have a high level of respect, trust and confidence in their police department."

• One of the more specific goals aimed at achieving that vision: "Provide neighborhood security and solve neighborhood problems."

• Three measures that would relate to whether the department was successfully achieving that goal: "Percent [of citizens] who frequently observed illegal gang activity,"

20

hard statistics on property crimes, and citizen survey data on how well the department followed up on reported problems in a neighborhood.

But for theory to impact reality, the development of any performance measurement hierarchy has to lead to a change in behavior of the organization that is the object of the exercise, and that doesn't always happen. Again, we could digress into a protracted discussion on theories of organizational dynamics and innovation, but let's not. Suffice it to say that some organizations are so insular, backwards, defensive, small-minded, turf-happy and paranoid that they're never going to change; others have the right mix of trust, leadership, desperation and resources (not necessarily monetary, but that sure helps) to forge ahead.

Happily, the Long Beach P.D. fell into the latter category. And so based on this whole exercise, the police department started doing things differently: Police officers began to reach out to the community by, among other things, getting out of their police cars more, and not just to gather information on a crime. They began to work on crime prevention by more sophisticated targeting of crime patterns. And in general they started deploying staff and equipment much more strategically and proactively. And they started winning.

In the five years following the departmental shift to a focus on performance—1991 to 1995—violent crime in Long Beach tumbled 38 percent, property crime dropped 19 percent and "gang-related incidents" fell nearly 40 percent. At the same time, the percentage of citizens who said they felt safe in their neighborhoods went from 50 percent in 1993 (the year the city began surveying citizens) to 64 percent in 1995.

It can be argued that crime statistics in general had started to go down nationwide starting in the early 1990s, and so Long Beach was just being carried along by the national societal trend. But Long Beach was outperforming the national numbers in all categories. And if one takes into account its previous performance as the starting point for improvement, the percentage gains are even more impressive. Now that's either a very amazing coincidence, or Long Beach, in focusing on results, had started to do some things right.

Chapter One Quick Quiz

1. You know it's a good time to consider a comprehensive performance measurement program when:
   a. "unresponsive, inflexible and ineffectual" are the nice things that people have to say about your organization.
   b. you learn that your city council is thinking about contracting out your jobs to local Boy Scout Troop 824.
   c. you've been ordered to.

2. A good first step in a performance measurement program might be to:
   a. talk to your "customers" and find out what they want from you (and, by extension, what it is you ought to be doing).
   b. spend months arguing over the definition of "customer."
   c. decide you don't have customers, just owners, and if government's not working very well, it's obviously the owners' fault.

3. A good second step in a performance measurement program might be to:
   a. come up with some vision/mission statement with which to focus your performance measurement effort.
   b. put your hands over your eyes.
   c. schedule an appointment with your ophthalmologist.

4. A good third step in a performance measurement program might be to:

    a. develop a dozen or so more specific goals that will move you toward fulfilling your overall mission/vision statement.

    b. develop a dozen or so good reasons why you can't do performance measurement (see Chapter 2).

    c. develop that roll of film that's been sitting in your camera since Christmas.

5. A good fourth step in a performance measurement program might be to:

    a. come up with a good list of results-based indicators/measures under each of your goals that will allow you to track your progress—or lack thereof—toward those goals over time.

    b. come up with a list of those in your office most likely to run for cover when upper management asks for volunteers to help with this.

    c. come up with a list of things you need at the store.

The Long Beach P.D.'s 14-Step Plan for Kicking the Losing Habit

Goals to Meet Community Needs

- Focus on community priorities
- Improve community access to the police department
- Develop new partnerships

Goals to Improve Customer Service

- Improve patrol response time
- Reduce illegal gang activity
- Provide effective criminal investigations
- Reduce illegal drug activity
- Provide neighborhood security and solve neighborhood problems
- Reduce prostitution and lewd behavior
- Improve traffic safety

Goals to Improve Support Services

- Improve services that support patrol and investigations

Goals to Maximize the Use of Department Resources

- Maximize the effectiveness of human resources
- Leverage existing and emerging technologies
- Maximize the effective use of vehicles and equipment

A Government Official's Guide to Customers

I t was with the advent of Total Quality Management that the concept of "customer" began strongly infusing the public management lexicon—a key concept of TQM being that customer satisfaction is the ultimate gauge of performance. This has caused lots of arguments among students and practitioners of government alike over who is and isn't a customer of government, or whether government can even *have* customers.

The reason that the word has caused so much consternation in public sector circles is that "customer" implies a narrow and one-way relationship that resonates with subservience: Businesses try to please customers; indeed, their very survival depends on pleasing their customers.

And so it is easy to see how the concept might be tough to apply comfortably in the public sector. Are welfare recipients customers of a state or local social services department? If they are customers, then why are we trying to get them off welfare? Shouldn't we be upping their assistance and never demanding that they do a lick of work in their lives?

Or if citizens are all customers, are they then absolved of all responsibility for the ultimate health and efficiency of the overall governmental enterprise? Are citizen-customers simply passive consumers of a big product: government?

Obviously, though, "customer" in a public-sector sense doesn't mean quite the same thing as in the private sector. "Customer" is more of stand-in term for anybody government is serving or dealing with in a direct way. So a key point to make here is that when government serves its "customers," the goal isn't always necessarily to make them happy, nor should it be inferred that in calling citizens "customers," citizens are absolved from their larger responsibilities to society.

When the term "customer" comes up in a law enforcement or regulatory setting, for example, it is important not to take the term as literally as if it were being applied to the purchase of french fries at the local Grease 'n' Go. As the director of one state corrections department summed it up: "Yes, prisoners are my customers. But in my case, the customer is not always right." In Madison, Wisconsin, the police department even considers criminals a type of "customer," albeit a type from which the cops don't solicit repeat business.

Furthermore, it's not always the public that government serves. Administrative agencies in government usually serve governmental customers. And some governmental entities can have many types of customers. A government personnel office, for example, has to consider the needs of other government agencies, the needs of government employees and the needs of those interested in finding jobs in government. And so some governmental entities distinguish between "inside" and "outside" customers, or "primary" and "secondary" customers.

For other government functions, such as departments of motor vehicles or licensing boards, "customer" fits more comfortably in the traditional retail sense of the word, although, again, it can still be nuanced where enforcement of rules and regulations is an issue.

And so "customer" may not be the perfect, or most palatable, word to use for those whom some government agency or office deals with or serves day in and day out. However, it's a handy word, and does remind government that it exists, in many ways, to serve.

So rather than argue about the word, it's probably a better idea to figure out who it is you as a governmental entity are supposed to be helping—or even overseeing—on a day-to-day basis and then figure out how to do that most efficiently and effectively, keeping in mind the highest principles of a collective citizenry and a healthy society as you go about your business.

Finally, there are those who legitimately worry about the impact on the attitude of the average American upon discovering that they've become "customers" of their governments instead of "citizens" within them. The fear is that Americans are going to simply belly up to government and start demanding service.

So a final admonition in case there are any non-government-employee-type citizens reading this book: Don't get the idea that just because certain parts of government are starting to view you in some instances as a "customer," you're absolved from getting off your backside and working in whatever way you can—by voting, volunteering, running for office or whatever—to support and even improve government. After all, you do own it.

(For an excellent discussion of "customer" and an excellent guide to surveying customers, it's worth shelling out $23.50 for a copy of *Customer Surveys for Agency Managers*, by Harry P. Hatry, et. al., by the Urban Institute Press. To order: 800-462-6420.)

CHAPTER TWO

Eight Reasons Why You Can't Do Performance Measurement and Then the One Reason Why You Have No Choice

Rather than dive immediately into the details of how to do performance measurement in the public sector, it's first worth considering all the reasons why you can't possibly do performance measurement *especially* in the public sector...or all the reasons that those around you will use to argue why you can't. Let's take them in the order in which they'll be encountered:

REASON NUMBER 1: We already did that.

Well, not exactly.
First you did Program Planning Budgeting. That sank

out of sight for the very simple reason that nobody had any idea what "program planning budgeting" meant. Plus it was too hard for anyone to say three times fast.

Next you did Zero Based Budgeting. ZBB operated on the theory that every budget cycle was the dawning of a new day. Now, if you're running a lemonade stand, that might be a feasible way to handle your budget. If you're running a slightly more complex entity, say the United States Department of Defense, ZBB would essentially require that you devote something like 364 days of your fiscal year to the budget process and one day a year to maintaining world peace.

ZBB having sunk out of sight, you did Management by Objectives. As near as anyone can figure out, Management by Objectives was an exercise whereby you sat down, figured out what you did that day, that week or that month, wrote that down on a piece of paper and submitted that piece of paper to your boss. That piece of paper then went into your file. The file went into your boss's filing cabinet. The filing cabinet is now sitting in a government surplus furniture warehouse somewhere in Sunderland, Maryland.

MBO was replaced by a much more formidable management reform potion: Total Quality Management. Now, to be fair, TQM has been given a bum rap, basically on account of the fact that it traveled so closely on the heels of such a complete loser as MBO. Also, those pushing TQM had a cult-like devotion to it that naturally turned a lot of people off. Plus, folks were orchestrating elaborate TQM efforts to figure out such things as: If Department of Motor Vehicle window attendants in South Carolina were given more change in their cash drawers at the beginning of the day, making change would be less of a problem as the day wore on. Or if mental hospital patients in California were given plastic utensils instead of metal ones, fewer staff members would be getting stabbed in the leg. And so forth. But the fact is, the more common-sense concepts associated with TQM, such as focusing on your customer and gathering the right data to gauge the effectiveness of your operation, are the fundamentals of performance measurement.

Meanwhile, there's already a new *post*-performance measurement trend. It's called "The Balanced Scorecard." Don't be alarmed, though, because the Balanced Scorecard is actually just a variation on performance measurement. In essence, it focuses performance measurement in four areas: *customer service* (sound familiar?); *financial accountability* (see "efficiency and effectiveness" discussion, Chapter Six); *internal work efficiencies* (see discussion of performance-based management, Chapter Eight); and *learning and growth*.

While the first three seem similar to what other governments are doing with regard to performance measurement, the "learning and growth" component of the Balanced Scorecard is somewhat intriguing. Implicit in any performance measurement effort, one would hope, is that staff will be trained and equipment upgraded as necessary to improve performance (actually, one would hope that would be implicit when it comes to doing or running anything, regardless of the management technique du jour). Under the Balanced Scorecard, the training and technology components are made explicit—that to continually improve, staff *will* be given regular and targeted training (in contrast to the traditional school of training known as "counting butts in chairs"), and technology *will* be upgraded. Unfortunately, not many governments have a whole lot of surplus cash to blow on new technology or training, which is why in most jurisdictions the "Slightly Off Kilter Scorecard" school of performance measurement will likely continue to dominate.

REASON NUMBER 2: Performance measures are inherently unfair because I only have so much control over outcomes.

The trickiest part of performance measurement—indeed its very accessible Achilles' heel—is that in a lot of areas of government activity and involvement, it's hard to say with absolute certainty that because government did this, that happened. Was it jail time or the drug rehab program that put Jack or Jane back on the straight and narrow (and how long did they stay there, anyway?). Does mandatory kindergarten improve a kid's ability to learn in later life, or does it merely increase the chances that he'll soon be transmitting the latest flu virus to the whole family?

The connection gets even harder to make when one considers that the ultimate results of many government actions won't be known for a long time. After all, the real measure of success for children who've spent 12 years in public school is that they're able to deal with life's vicissitudes with equilibrium and confidence as they grow older, not that they scored a combined 1208 on their SATs.

The cause-and-effect and long-term-consequences conundra of performance measurement are two of the clubs with which its critics most frequently and happily beat it up. (The other club is the apples-versus-oranges argument, which we'll get to later.)

The cause-and-effect puzzle is best illustrated by a recent phenomenon that has a lot of people paying attention to government performance: The startling reduction in the crime rate in New York City over the past few years. The city has witnessed double-digit drops in crime through the 1990s. The reductions have come in all categories, petty to felonious. In terms of cause and effect, however, the city is a performance measurement proponent's simultaneous dream and nightmare. Clearly, there are some excellent results there: People on the street even say they feel safer, which is what some in law enforcement argue is the ultimate desired result of any public safety effort.

The nightmare part comes in explaining the reasons for the drop. Was the reduction the result of former police Commissioner Bill Bratton's "no-tolerance" law enforcement policy, which had beat cops citing people for everything from littering to playing their radios too loudly (Bratton's plausible theory being that allowing a little anarchy only serves to encourage a lot of it)? Was it a result of the city's newly computerized crime-tracking system, which the force says has allowed it to deploy its anti-crime resources with top efficiency? Was it the result of the department's restructured management system, which has overhauled the department's bureaucracy in a way that the top brass argue now has the whole force working together in a more cooperative, collaborative way? Or is it all merely the result of an improving economy and fewer juveniles and young adults living in the city?

Alan Altshuler, director of the Taubman Center for State and Local Government at Harvard's John F. Kennedy School of Government, argues that the actions of the police department have to be credited in large part with the impressive result. John DiIulio, a public policy professor at Princeton, will swear equally hard that economics, demographics and the role of community in supporting childhood development are what's critical.

But just to complicate matters, it's possible that both Altshuler and DiIulio are wrong. The real reason for the reduction might be something the city did way back when. Maybe some long-forgotten family assistance or education or economic development program that popped up and then disappeared a dozen or so years ago has finally paid off in a multi-year string of dramatically lower rates of crime.

As you can see, it's easy to get hung up on the cause-and-effect argument. Getting hung up is made easier still by those governments that have included in their performance measures things that they obviously don't have much power over at all. One of Minnesota's goals, as stated in its "Minnesota Milestones" report of 1992, was to increase the life expectancy of its residents from 77.9 years to 85.2 by the year 2020. Arguably, there are so many factors influencing life expectancy—from personal habits to genetics to serendipity—that it's pretty implausible, if not a bit arrogant, to suppose that state policy can directly influence this one.

The whole social services world best represents how tough, on the one hand, and easy, on the other, it can be to connect cause and effect. In the wake of welfare reform, for example, there's been a huge debate over why people have dropped off the rolls. Good economy? Too much of a hassle to stay on assistance? Effective welfare-to-work efforts? The debate is on and won't be settled for a while. On the other hand, a more aggressive approach to both establishing paternity and going after deadbeat dads is clearly having an impact on the financial well-being of an increasing number of women, and states and counties have the data to prove that.

Yet the argument that we can never know for sure exactly what affects socio-economic trends or human behavior—or that it is too often forces beyond our control that are having the impact—is, for some people, reason enough to drop the whole performance measurement idea. But that's an argument that just isn't washing anymore.

A growing cadre of public policy officials and experts now argue that in the face of such unknowables and such unanswerables as those surrounding cause and effect, the best thing to do is to forge ahead. In fact, they're arguing that we're way past due for forging ahead—that it's about time government started getting serious about gathering performance data so that some long-term analyses of cause and effect can finally begin. Why hundreds of thousands of people dropped off the rolls in the wake of welfare reform is not some unsolvable mystery destined to be lost to the ages; it's just going to take some time and focus to get at the answer. (Of course, a whole bunch of politicians already have the answer: "Thank me!")

And the fact is, gauging cause and effect needn't always be a long-term or hopelessly subjective endeavor. Let's return to New York City and Bratton's high-profile and very concrete program to cut crime. New York's performance has been dramatic enough to get the attention of dozens of other cities. Indeed, soon after being squeezed out of his job in New York by Mayor Rudy Giuliani (one of the dicier issues around performance measurement isn't *only* who gets the *blame* for the bad numbers; it's also who gets *credit* for the good numbers), Bratton started consulting for the long-time crime-rate basket case, New Orleans, on how to replicate the New York City phenomenon. Certainly the dramatic numbers in New York make the experiment worth a shot, and early returns from New Orleans indicate that Brattonism translates well. In the Big Easy, long known for crooked cops and dangerous streets, trends are now swinging the Big Apple way.

But if some still argue that the cause-and-effect argument is not cinched by the New Orleans experiment, one thing is certain: Nobody will be able to gauge the impact of government action one way or the other without at least first developing the standards by which performance will be judged, and then by collecting and analyzing some baseline data.

Just as obviously, there are those areas of policy where cause and effect can't be connected overnight. In such instances, the mere act of measuring performance may not change anything at first. But as governments begin to develop performance indicators—and, it is hoped, begin standardizing those indicators across jurisdictions—there will be a growing pool of cross-referenceable data that presumably will allow analysts to begin vectoring in more accurately on where cause and effect does exist. It may be that in some areas, government finds it can do very little to impact outcomes; in others, it might be able to do quite a bit. Either way, those are both very good things for government to know.

REASON NUMBER 3: Performance measures are going to be used to beat me up, not help me out.

This is a very legitimate worry. The traditional managerial mindset is: "You screw up; I punish you." Now, we could go the pop-psychology best-seller route here and try to analyze the roots of this mindset, but you know where that leads and, let's face it, we've blamed enough on our parents without doing it in a book on public administration. The point is, in measuring performance, higher-ups will be tempted to revel in newfound ways to slap underlings around. The other point is, you don't want to be on the receiving end of any of that. How do you avoid it? You do what other smart public officials are doing and use performance data to turn the tables, and we're going to cap this chapter with the story of Charlie Deane, chief of police in Prince William County, Virginia, who did just that.

REASON NUMBER 4: Performance measurement is going to invite unfair comparison.

This is the apples-vs.-oranges criticism of performance measurement. It is the one that inspires a good deal of the fear about the practice among managers, and for a simple reason: A high-profile consequence of broad performance measurement efforts nationwide will likely be that as governments and government agencies start to collect performance data, performance of like agencies increasingly is going to be compared from one jurisdiction to the next. Why is a greater proportion of serious crimes solved in Arlington, Virginia, than in San Antonio, Texas? Why is the cost of fire protection per capita so much higher in Cincinnati, Ohio, than in Wichita, Kansas? Why do veterans' hospitals in Pennsylvania seem to do such a better job of caring for patients who suffer from such chronic ailments as diabetes and obstructive pulmonary disease than veterans' hospitals in Southern California? Why do pedestrians get mowed down by cars in Orlando, Florida, at a higher rate than in Boston, Massachusetts?

One need only watch the recriminations fly after *Money* magazine publishes its thoroughly silly but widely read "Best Places to Live" issue each year to know how sensitive public officials are to this sort of high-visibility comparison. And that's fluffy stuff. Think of what happens when the comparisons are legitimate. Which is why the International City/County Management Association has had a little tougher time than it expected in launching its ambitious and praiseworthy Center for Performance Measurement. While the center's main function is to help cities and counties develop performance measures across key functions, one product of the effort is the publication of an annual data report that compares the performance of participating jurisdictions across those functional areas. ICMA has found that it is the "comparison" portion of the program with which participating cities and counties have the most trouble. Jurisdictions are happy to learn how to improve their own performance; they're not wild about having that performance compared with anybody else's.

There are three separate branches of the apples-versus-oranges (-versus-grapes) complaint. The first is that it is unfair to compare the performance of places that are just plain socio-economically or demographically different. The second is that it is unfair to compare the performance of places that are different for reasons of geography. The third is that different jurisdictions may do their measuring differently, and so one might end up looking better than another only because of what's being measured and the way data are gathered and interpreted and not because of actual performance. Let's take these on in order:

Poor people are poor performers: The complaint about socio-economic differences has deep roots and tends to get very emotional. For years, many public policy experts have argued that socio-economically disadvantaged jurisdictions are going to look really bad in comparisons with jurisdictions of privilege when it comes to measuring everything from cleanliness to crime, and that that's not fair. This goofy form of opposition to performance measurement is rooted in American public policy analysts' tradition of handicapping results based on circumstances.

For an illustration of how deeply rooted this tradition is, consider a meeting that was held in Washington, D.C., a few years ago, during which a group of state, local and federal public policy experts gathered to discuss the possibility of developing broad performance measures across a host of state, local and federal government functions. The discussion traveled in familiar circles, with participants endlessly arguing definitions, jockeying for political and intellectual position by trumpeting past career triumphs and dropping high-powered names and affiliations, and, very occasionally, actually addressing the topic at hand. But one participant in particular was adamant in opposing the idea of performance measurement, and the reason was based on this whole concept of national civic inequality. Inasmuch as performance measurement invited comparison, this learned personage argued, it just wasn't fair to compare the performance of, for example, an inner-city school system with a suburban one.

This argument seems to be based on the notion that performance measurement is somehow an end in itself; those who perform well get a gold star; those who perform poorly will be relegated to the corner, dunce cap and all. The new (and apparently radical) view, by contrast, is that perhaps reasons for poor performance—including socio-economic reasons—should be confronted and addressed and not masked by some form of performance measurement handicapping.

It's the snow's fault: Thwarted there, critics of performance measurement will turn to geography. How can you compare the performance of police in Little Rock with those in Minneapolis? Response times in Minneapolis, after all, may be hampered by ice and snow. On the other hand, Little Rock never has those crime-dulling, weeks-long, sub-zero cold snaps; what it has instead are those temper-shortening, 100-plus heat waves. Or one official will argue that there's no public transportation in my upstate county, so how can I get welfare recipients to jobs? While another complains that there's tons of public transportation in my city, but all the jobs are in the suburbs. And on and on it can go in a cycle

37

of comparison avoidance that lots of folks are happy to ride forever. They are happy to ride it forever because it allows them to avoid having to address the problems and issues that a real hard look at performance might require.

Those guys set the bar low, but we set it high: Finally, opponents complain that you can't compare jurisdictions that do their measuring differently. Governmental pioneers in performance measurement don't have much patience for that argument either, and are already preempting such criticism by actually doing the performance comparisons themselves. Portland, Oregon, for example, regularly rates itself against six other comparable jurisdictions in fundamental areas of local government performance, from public safety to sewer and water service. By doing the comparison itself, the city ensures that what is measured and how it is measured are consistent across jurisdictions.

And while it might make some jurisdictions squeamish, the International City/County Management Association launched its performance measurement center in part on the very solid theory that comparing the performance of like jurisdictions has tremendous value, particularly when it comes to learning about how other jurisdictions do various things well (120 cities and counties have signed on to the ICMA effort so far). The corollary, while perhaps distasteful, is worth stating here: A jurisdiction may be cruising along thinking that it's doing one heck of a job, when in fact there may be lots of room for improvement. And if they'd just look next door, or a couple of states over, they'd find that out.

The problem, says Scott Bryant, who you'll remember from Chapter One as one of the internal consultants in Long Beach during the police department overhaul, is that quite a few jurisdictions would prefer *not* to find that out. "One of the big problems in pushing performance measurement is that as long as you don't know how your performance compares—and as long as nobody else knows—there's no pressure to change."

Which is why those jurisdictions that are brave enough

to have signed on to the ICMA effort—and agreed to have their performance data published next to that of other cities and counties—deserve a lot of credit. But let's cut to the chase, and it's this: Once a critical mass of jurisdictions begins to produce half-decent statistics on performance in certain key areas—whether it's data on internal administration or data on things that the general public cares about, such as law enforcement or education—the comparisons are going to start flying anyway. Just look at what already happens when the FBI releases the latest Uniform Crime Report statistics. Those numbers are gobbled up by the press the moment they come out as reporters quickly calculate their own city's ranking in the crime-fighting sweepstakes. Likewise for national educational test results and even fire department response times. And before you know it, some enterprising reporter—that is, some reporter who isn't running around Washington, D.C., trying to ferret out such vital information as who is sleeping with whom—is going to crack the ICMA data book and ask what really is a much more interesting question: Why are people in Houston happier with their street lighting than people in San Jose?

The fact is, such issues as who has the most efficient social services system, the smartest kids, the best cops, the quickest snowplows, the cleanest drinking water or even the most reliable street lighting are of intense interest to citizens. And pretty soon, jurisdictions not producing performance data in such areas are going to be asked why they're not.

REASON NUMBER 5: Performance measurement is a great idea, but it's down the tubes when this administration gets tossed out of office.

Political time lines do foment against performance measurement efforts—and any other management reform efforts, for that matter. Politicians may understandably be reluctant to invest in a major, long-term performance measurement effort, given that there is probably not going to be a whole lot of short-term political payoff. The mayor of Noblesville, Indiana, Mary Sue Rowland, successfully shepherded through an impressive and very detailed city-wide performance measurement effort in the early 1990s. Her thanks: a primary election defeat based on an issue entirely unrelated to performance measurement.

Furthermore, even good ideas have a nasty tendency to get tossed out when a new regime sweeps in. The nation's bellwether performance measurement effort—Oregon Benchmarks—has certainly had its ups and downs because of political turnover (though Oregon deserves a lot of credit for ultimately sticking with the program).

But while politics will certainly continue to be one of the principle reasons why performance measurement doesn't fly in a lot of places (or gets shot down halfway off the tarmac), it is also one of the big reasons why it *does* fly in others, and there are some basic reasons for that. First, taxpayers aren't getting any less cranky about what they ante up each year to government; they're very curious about what their tax money is buying, and they want detailed information about that. Meanwhile, a growing number of politicians—particularly local politicians—are coming around to the idea that performance measurement makes good management sense, which makes good political sense. And the fact is, performance measurement *can* make good political sense. Rudy Giuliani has been rendered just plain politically invincible by the crime-fighting stats coming out of the Big Apple; Mayor Marc Morial of New Orleans is considering altering the city charter so he can run for a third term, riding a wave of tumbling crime statistics in his city.

Nevertheless, the larger problem of the politicians' role in performance measurement certainly can't be dismissed. Many of them—particularly legislators—don't really understand performance measurement, and that represents a serious long-term impediment to effective implementation.

If you ask upper-level career managers in the federal government to assess Congress's performance when it comes to shepherding the Government Performance and Results Act along, you'll get an earful about the micromanaging fatheads that Congress has assigned to monitor departmental progress, fatheads who seem more interested in controlling the process than in encouraging implementation.

But that's the nature of legislatures (particularly national legislatures), and probably comes under the heading of "live with it." The most that anyone involved in a performance measurement effort can probably do is pray that legislators—federal, state or local—will at least try to learn something about the practice and will at least consider turning to performance measures when it comes to evaluating programs and budgets (but, of course, only *after* they've turned to their largest campaign contributors for their invaluable guidance and advice).

REASON NUMBER 6: There's no way to measure what I do.

This argument cuts two ways, neither of which is going to buy you anything by way of relief. First, if there really is no way to measure the impact of what you do, it may be that what you're doing isn't contributing much to the overall governmental enterprise and you should turn your attention and energy to something that does contribute.

Second, as the alchemy of performance measurement has progressed, proponents have begun getting pretty creative in developing workable performance indicators, either indicators that really do measure ultimate effectiveness, or "surrogate" or "intermediate" indicators that can stand in as pretty good predictors of more bottom-line results (more on surrogate measures later). Plus there are new technologies that are making the whole measurement proposition much more feasible (although the cost and quality of the technology that's out there still can be a significant stumbling block to implementing an effective measurement effort).

But the bottom line is this: It will probably only take you a couple of phone calls to learn of somebody else who is applying performance measures to exactly what you do (if what you're doing is, indeed, worth doing).

That is why an entire chapter—Chapter Five—of this book is devoted to "measuring the unmeasurable." The chapter outlines examples of governments measuring performance in areas from international relations to social services to economic development, all of which in the old days were considered performance measurement-proof.

REASON NUMBER 7: My agency/department/division has conflicting missions.

Some governmental entities do, in fact, have conflicting missions, which makes measuring progress toward some overarching goal kind of tough. The U.S. General Accounting Office points out (in one of its many reports on how poorly the feds are doing in their progress on the Government Performance and Results Act) that the U.S. Forest Service, for example, is supposed to see to the efficient killing of trees and the careful protection of wildlife. So, asks the report, what is it that the USFS ought to be measuring in judging its effectiveness?

In such a case, the Forest Service is probably justified in telling Congress that GPRA is a great little law in theory, but that, pending clarification of its mission, the USFS is going to take a pass on complying with it. Not that Congress is unaware of the USFS dilemma. Another recent GAO report addressed to Senator Frank H. Murkowski, a Republican from Alaska who chairs the Senate Committee on Energy and Natural Resources, spells out the dilemma with admirable clarity. In order for the USFS to become an efficient organization, says *Forest Service Decision-Making: A Framework for Improving Performance*, the USFS must "strengthen accountability for performance." Before it can do that, the report hastens to add, somebody is going to have to deal with the fact that "agreement does not exist on the agency's long-term strategic goals," and therefore on what ought to be measured in accounting for USFS's progress toward those goals, improved or otherwise.

Of course this particular policy area is a political hot potato. Environmentalists think the USFS should dedicate itself to saving every banana slug in the forest. The timber industry wants the USFS to run roads into virgin stands of timber so that they can all be reduced to the ecological equivalent of a Wal-Mart parking lot. Knowing Congress's ability to handle such tough issues in a timely fashion, Pee-Wee Herman will be Speaker of the House before this particular conflict gets resolved.

The fact is, though, not as many governmental entities fall into the USFS category as claim to. Even the U.S. Department of Defense, part of whose job is to sometimes kill folks in large quantities, can safely argue that its ultimate goal is peace.

REASON NUMBER 8: I still don't feel like it.

The truth is that some form of prolonged filibuster against performance measurement will probably ultimately work if there is a critical mass of resistance to the idea in your department or division or office. As an upper-level manager at the U.S. Department of Agriculture notes: "I would say, quite frankly, that the jury is still out on [GPRA]. The one difference between PPB and ZBB and GPRA is that GPRA *is* law. That makes it a little harder to ignore, but not impossible."

And the fact is that it's unlikely that Congress is either going to yank anybody's appropriation or ask the president to call out the Air Force in an effort to enforce compliance with GPRA. Nor are state and local government career staff unfamiliar with the strategy of running out the clock on the latest management fad. In fact, the veterans are really very good at it.

Rather than fight it, though, there is another, less cynical way to view performance measurement, and that is to figure out what it might be able to do for you, rather than to you. There are some people who are actually using the momentum of performance measurement to get more funding for their agencies; to win some flexibility from dumb rules and regulations; to streamline overall operations; and to force legislative bodies to begin taking some responsibility for the conflicting directives or whimsy-driven laws and budgets that they seem to have such a good time passing.

Now, we needn't be unrealistic here about the possibility that performance measurement is somehow going to wind up being some broad back avenue to reforming your own shop or to forcing your legislature to get real. However, you have been handed a somewhat large stick; it might be that the best course of action is to give somebody a sharp shot in the shins with it.

Charlie Deane, chief of police in Prince William County, Virginia, used performance measurement to give his county board of supervisors a light tap not so long ago, and it worked. After being criticized in a performance audit for his department's apparently poor showing with regard to clearing cases, Deane turned around and used the numbers to prove to the county board that his performance was actually pretty good given that his was one of the most understaffed and overworked county police departments in the region.

He got more money for new officers.

Which brings us back to Reason Number 3 for not wanting to pursue performance measurement: that a poor showing will only mean a public upbraiding for shoddy work, as opposed to being the catalyst for some reasoned discussion and debate about how to improve performance (including perhaps winning additional resources). The fact is, smart managers—as Deane proved—turn the tables. The key to his success in doing that, though, was that he didn't attack the practice of performance measurement as somehow being unfair and he didn't filibuster against it; instead, he embraced performance measurement as a legitimate management (and political) exercise and used results to get what he needed.

So start embracing, because even though arguing the pros and cons of performance measurement is lots of fun, and even though you've been subjected to countless, cascading come-and-go management fads for the past 30 years, this time it's a moot point. Chances are that when performance measurement rolls your way, it won't be an optional exercise.

In fact, if you're a federal employee, performance measurement is *already* not an optional exercise, thanks to GPRA, which lots of folks were hoping Congress would simply forget all about, awash as it has been in such important matters as PennyantelanddealinArkansasgate and BillGates. However, Congress, led by some heavy hitters such as House Majority Leader Dick Armey, appears to have rediscovered GPRA. So, given that GPRA was signed by a Democratic president and is now being enforced by a Republican Congress, it looks like the practice has finally arrived for real at the federal level...after having first been proposed by Teddy Roosevelt in 1909.

At the state and local level, performance measurement is still optional in most places, but that probably won't be the case for long. At some point in the next few years, the Governmental Accounting Standards Board, which sets all accounting rules for state and local government, will likely make "Service Efforts and Accomplishments Reporting" mandatory. ("Service Efforts and Accomplishments Reporting," for those not versed in the jargon of public accounting, is the two-dollar term that governmental accounting types use to mean that governments will have to start reporting on what they are doing to achieve certain public goals and how close they're coming to succeeding. In other words, they're going to have to start measuring performance.)

Because every level of government is—or is soon going to have to be—reporting on performance, you now have no choice but to read Chapter 3...and it's a dense one.

Chapter Two Quick Quiz

1. A good reason *not* to do performance measurement would be:
   a. I don't want to know how we're doing.
   b. I don't want my boss or anybody else to know how we're doing.
   c. I think we're doing a great job.

2. A good reason *to* do performance measurement would be:
   a. there is the off chance that the higher-ups in my organization will take this seriously and may actually reward me for good performance with increased resources and a raise.
   b. there is the off chance that the higher-ups in my organization will take this seriously and may actually try to get me some additional help if it turns out that my performance suffers due to a lack of resources.
   c. waiting it out might not work this time.

3. Once you've embarked on your performance measurement effort it is probably realistic *not* to expect that:
   a. your legislative body will use the data as a starting point for productive discussion of whether you've got enough resources to do your job well.

b. some politician will publicly praise you for being brave enough to expose yourself to this kind of scrutiny.

c. the press will do a thoughtful and heart-warming story on how your department is using performance data in an effort to reconnect government and citizens.

4. Once you've embarked on your performance measurement effort, it is probably reasonable *to* expect that:

a. your council/legislature/board/commission will ignore the whole effort until budget time rolls around, and when budget time does roll around, you'll be asked to cut yours by 5 percent.

b. some politician or other is going to use your results to further his/her career.

c. the press will completely misinterpret the data you deliver to them and proceed to beat you black and blue on the front page of the local paper.

CHAPTER THREE

You Win. What Is It?

T he great thing about management trends is all the different terms that experts invent to go with them. These terms serve a clear and useful purpose: to confuse people. The more confused people are, the less likely they are to ask good, hard questions about any of this stuff. Consultants, in particular, like this feature of management trends, except in their case it's because the more confused people are, the less likely they are to ask for their money back. Academics like all the different terms because it allows them to argue over definitions, which is what academics spend 80 percent of their waking hours doing (they spend the other 20 percent organizing conferences at which to argue about definitions).

So this chapter will be devoted to explaining what performance measurement is and to deciphering some of the key definitions swirling around the practice.

GOVERNMENTS HAVE ALWAYS been really good at measuring one thing: spending; bureaucrats can follow that bouncing dollar as if it were radioactive. Consequently, budget decisions have tended to be driven mostly by how much an agency was given to spend in the previous fiscal year. Lately, governments have been getting better at measuring one other thing, too: action; that is, what sort of activity the spending supports (spending doesn't qualify as an "action," here; counseling somebody on getting off welfare and into work does).

What government has been really lousy at is measuring what was accomplished through that spending and action. For example, social services agencies have long been able to report in great detail what their annual budgets are and for what programs the money was parceled out. Quite a few of them now can also report in decent detail such things as how many hours case managers spent helping move clients from welfare to work (and how many clients were thus served). What they haven't been able to tell anybody in any meaningful detail is whether those clients were better off as a result of all that spending and serving. The United States Department of State can report in great detail how much it spends on overseas missions annually and, indeed, how many ambassadors it has assigned worldwide. What it hasn't been able to report was whether the U.S. or the world was any better off for the outlay or for having all those people in striped pants running around the globe.

The reason for the abundance of data on spending and activity, on the one hand, versus impact, on the other, is obvious: It's easy to track money spent, along with such tangibles as clients served or ambassadorships filled; it's harder to track such less-tangibles as improved lives or safer worlds. But that's the ultimate goal of performance measurement: to refocus government—in management and budgeting along with program and policy development—on those kinds of bottom-line results.

But before we even get into such large issues as the whys and wherefores of what governments do or don't measure or should or shouldn't measure, it is first necessary to turn some attention to the daunting but vital issue of definitions. One of the chief reasons that performance measurement has proved such an elusive target is that when it comes to implementing it in government, everybody seems to be using similar words in different ways (or different words in similar ways). And while this may keep consultants and academics happy, it's sort of wearing on the poor schmo who actually has to try to make this stuff work.

The high-in-the-chapter disclaimer is that nailing down definitions around performance measurement once and for all probably isn't actually possible. Everybody in the performance measurement game, it seems, has a slightly different take on what the words mean, how they ought to be used and how they fit together. And when it comes to hairsplitting around definitions, performance measurement gurus have it down to a fine art. The main aim of this chapter, then, is to present the essential concepts behind performance measurement using what seems to be the most commonly accepted word usage with the understanding that we're just trying to get readers into the definitional ballpark. Here goes.

The Magnificent Seven

For now we'll look only at the very basic words that underpin performance measurement. Seven terms are of particular importance. They are: *mission, goals, outcome indicator, activity, output, input and efficiency.* There is an eighth term that you are likely to be subjected to in the course of any investigation or discussion of performance measures; that word is *benchmark*, and we'll deal with it later in this chapter.

The trickiest thing about these definitions is that they're the verbal equivalent of fraternal septuplets: They're all closely related, and it's often easy to confuse them, but it's important to understand their various personalities so that you can begin to recognize them as separate and distinct.

you can begin to recognize them as separate and distinct. The easiest way to explain these seven main terms is to fold them all into an example. Now, if this were a cowardly book, we'd take as our example some governmental agency with a very simple mission, such as the National Aeronautics and Space Administration, whose mission is to hone hiding cost overruns into a fine art. But because we're bold, we'll take on the performance of a specific and very large federal department—the largest, in fact.

As required under the Government Performance and Results Act of 1993, every department in the federal government is going to have to submit annual performance plans to Congress. (Amazingly, Congress somehow inadvertently neglected to include *itself* under GPRA.) Naturally, one department that is going to have to submit such a performance plan is the Department of Defense. But in order for DoD to do that, it first must figure out what its basic job is. After all, it's pretty pointless to come up with a performance plan in the absence of any clear idea of what it is you're supposed to be achieving as an organization—your purpose in life. It is this broad goal of an organization that we refer to as its *mission*. That mission is often articulated in some sort of highfalutin' vision statement (as discussed briefly in Chapter One and as will be discussed in greater detail in Chapter Four).

But right off, life gets messy. Is it the Defense Department's mission to help maintain world peace? To fight and win wars? How about helping local, state or other federal law enforcement agencies in drug- or illegal-immigration interdiction? Or is the mission of DoD simply to test various advanced tactical weapons so that U.S. defense contractors can turn around and sell those weapons with confidence to other countries, thereby cutting the U.S. trade deficit and boosting U.S. economic security (but by doing so, also occasionally actually threatening world peace—wow, this does get messy)?

For the sake of our example, let's assume that DoD has,

after great soul-searching, decided that its core mission is not to be the equivalent of *Consumer Reports* for the defense industry, but rather to maintain a safe and secure world (it may have secondary missions, too, but this chapter is picky enough as it is without going into all that). Now we move to the next level of abstraction: *goals*. Goals are those slightly more specific areas of results that DoD wants to achieve that flow logically from *mission*. It's important to know that in some circles *goal*, *outcome* and *objective* are used interchangeably. It's not necessarily wrong to do that. But in the interest of foisting some order on the usage scene, we'll note that seasoned and competent veterans of performance measurement (there are a couple out there) DON'T use *goals*, *outcomes* or *objectives* interchangeably. Rather, *outcomes* and *objectives* represent a level of achievement just below goals—outcomes or objectives would be used to break goals down into even narrower, more measurable pieces (we'll see an example of this in Chapter Four when we discuss the U.S. Department of Education's strategic plan). Anyway, some goals related to DoD's overarching mission of maintaining world peace might include reducing regional conflicts worldwide, on the one hand, while seeing to it that U.S. fighting forces are combat-ready, on the other.

So DoD has a noble *mission*, and it has come up with more specific *goals* that flow from that mission. How does it gauge progress toward achieving those goals? Enter four kinds of performance measures: *outcome indicators*, *activities*, *outputs* and *inputs*.

We'll deal with *outcome indicators* first. *Outcome indicators* are the specific measures—the hard data, if you will—that allow an organization to assess its success in achieving (or at least moving toward) its *goals*. *Outcome indicators* related to the *goal* of reducing regional conflicts worldwide could include data on the number, length and severity of such conflicts, including information as specific as "number of casualties last year attributable to regional conflicts" or "number of civilians put in harm's way by of being combat-ready could include expert evaluation of the U.S. military's major weapons systems, the speed with which a battle fleet can deploy on short notice, or the collective target-shooting scores of the entire U.S. infantry. (Obviously, if a battle has to be joined, other rather more serious and immediate outcome indicators start coming into play that tell DoD very directly about its forces' fighting readiness.)

Mission, goal and *outcome indicator*, then, are the basic building blocks of a performance measurement system. If you've got a fairly good understanding of each of those, you're well on your way to being able to apply them yourself. So to review quickly: *Mission* is that overarching statement that describes an organization's reason for being. *Goals* are a first cut at dividing the mission up into slightly more tangible areas of measurability. *Outcome indicators* are the specific measures (the data) that tell you how well you're doing in achieving progress toward your goals and, by extension, your mission.

As we'll discuss later, it may not always be necessary to include all three levels—*mission, goal, outcome indicator*—in establishing a performance measurement system that works. It is possible, in some cases, to eliminate goals and skip right to outcome indicators if your mission is very simple. Or if it's obvious what you're supposed to be accomplishing, it may be OK to dispense with mission and just list some basic goals or objectives before you drop down to outcome indicator. On the other hand, if you're part of a very complex organization doing a very complicated job, you may need to add some layers—after *goals* you might want another layer that includes *outcomes* or *objectives*, or what have you—before you drop down to the very specific layer of outcome indicator. Again, it's more important to understand how outcome indicators feed into the more general goals and objectives of government programs and policies than it is to be locked slavishly into the hierarchy (or the words) outlined above.

With that in mind, let's forge ahead. The next three words that need to be covered as we tackle the performance measurement lexicon are *activity*, *outputs* and *inputs*, each of which causes immense headaches to both practitioners (like you) and those of us who try to explain this stuff (like me).

We'll look at *activity* and *outputs* first, and this is where we get into some serious hair-splitting. *Activities* are those actions that, presumably, are meant to move us toward a goal, outcome or objective. *Outputs* are the product or service being delivered through those actions. For example, if we're talking about a county social services department, then counseling somebody on finding a job is an *activity* related to the goal of moving people from welfare to self-sufficiency. The *output* is the number of people who receive counseling. Why separate the "activity" of counseling from the "output" of individuals counseled? Because it is sometimes helpful for managers to know all the steps involved in trying to achieve some output (and, by extension, some *outcome*), and in some cases there might be more than one activity involved; there might be lots of activities (trash haulers, for example, do a lot more than just pick up trash cans). By identifying all the discreet activities that build to delivering some output, managers (and workers) are then able to do a much more sophisticated analysis of the process by which certain things get done.

So how do *activities* and *outputs* relate to *outcome indicators*? In the welfare world, the activity of counseling supports the output of individuals counseled, which will influence the *outcome indicator* of "percentage of last quarter's caseload who now have jobs." Those data tell us how we're doing in achieving our *goal* of helping citizens move from public assistance to self-sufficiency.

So to continue our DoD example in explaining *activity* and *output*: Sending peace-keeping troops to the Middle East is an *activity* of DoD that results in the *output* of a peace-keeping mission. Both the *activity* and the *output* are meant to influence the *outcome indicator* of "number of casualties worldwide attributable to regional conflicts," which flows from the *goal* of "reducing regional conflicts worldwide." Buying the most technologically advanced tanks available is an *activity* that results in the *output* of dozens of really good tanks, which is related to the *outcome indicator* of being judged by experts as the most technologically advanced fighting force in the world, which flows from the *goal* of being combat-ready.

A more street-level example will probably help here: If you're in charge of a city sanitation department, a key *activity* is picking up garbage. An *output* might be the number of trash cans you've hoisted along your route, or the number of houses or businesses you've covered in a morning, or how many tons of trash you picked up that day. The *goal* is a pristine city. An *outcome indicator* related to that goal might be the number of free-range rats spotted over the course of a given two-week period in a sampling of alleys citywide, or the amount of trash seen skittering down roadways on any given blustery day.

If you're working in a state department of motor vehicles, one *activity* might be issuing a driver's license (the satisfied customer—the driver—and the driver's license itself would be *outputs*). Another activity might be NOT issuing a driver's license to somebody who can't see past the clerk's window, with or without glasses. One *goal* of the department might be to "support a safe, sane driving environment for all those who drive in the state." One *outcome indicator* related to that goal might be the number of road fatalities per thousand people in the state in a given year.

Which brings us, finally, down to the lowly but critical world of *inputs*. *Inputs* are the resources that go into creating any given *output*. Inputs can include the cost of such things as the labor, equipment, supplies, materials, building space, utilities and other overhead (including, naturally, the cost of that new hot-shot performance measurement consultant you're using right now) that culminate in a specific *output*.

Back to our DoD example: If the *output* is an incursion into a Middle East hot spot in order to rein in some despicable despot, then the *inputs* related to that *output* include the cost of soldiers (salaries, bennies and so forth) food, guns, transportation, fuel, ammo, and so on. *Inputs* could also plausibly include diplomatic support for the effort, such as embassy staff time and overhead apportioned to the mission. But it is very possible to get carried away in this exercise and try to include absolutely every possible related *input*. What is important is that an organization is able to get some sense of the basic costs of the major and obvious components that go into creating outputs. Having done that, and if you're very lucky, your organization might also actually be able to gauge in some less-than-vague way the cost of moving an *outcome indicator* (because, we assume, the outcome indicators are being directly influenced by activities and outputs, the cost of which we're calculating by measuring inputs). But to say that government is ever going to be able to directly link cost and outcomes is probably a stretch.

Now, all of that sounds hard and it sounds complicated, and it can be. But it is crucial to do if government is to keep its eye on that other objective that taxpayers so devoutly wish that government would work toward: *efficiency*.

Efficiency, which we'll delve into in much greater detail in Chapter Six, is based on the important assumption that the goal of government isn't simply to do things well but also to do those things at some reasonable cost. It's one thing to have a world-class water treatment plant; it's quite another if that world-class water is being delivered to you at a per-gallon price that renders it more valuable than a vintage Bordeaux. Being able to do some accurate cost accounting, therefore, is critical to the overall performance measurement equation. If you have no idea of what all of your key outputs are costing you, then it will be hard to gauge whether you're doing your job efficiently or not. Efficiency, to grossly simplify it, can be calculated by toting up the cost of the *inputs* that go into those *outputs* that underpin progress toward a goal, outcome or objective.

Again, this can be pretty simple to do if the task in question is, say, processing tax returns with 99.5 percent accuracy, or keeping garbage trucks rolling trouble-free, or handing out driver's licenses to all those who deserve them, or even moving somebody from welfare to work. It gets tougher to do when the goal is to cut down on regional conflicts around the world. In a gross way, DoD did, of course, calculate the cost of rushing troops to the Persian Gulf in order to bring a certain despicable despot to heel, and presumably that cost can be apportioned among soldiers' salaries, fuel, missiles, food, bullets, gas masks and so forth. The bottom line: It was a lot of money. (Some argue that school is still out on the results.)

Cutting Through the Jargon

Given the words and substitute words and the caveats to the words, it is understandable that people get confused by all of this. Indeed, this is probably the most discouraging chapter in this book (it certainly was discouraging for me to write; I'm still trying to figure all of this out). So a quick pep talk: It is easy to get bogged down in definition and confused about terminology. But if you talk to government officials who are gamely trying to implement performance measurement programs, what you quickly discover is that they refuse to get hung up on definitions or process. Rather, they cut to the core of what it is they're supposed to be accomplishing day in and day out, and then they forge ahead in figuring out some way to measure it.

If you ask somebody like Brian Wing, commissioner of the Office of Temporary and Disability Assistance for New York State, how he developed his performance measurement effort for a huge hunk of the state's huge social services world (an area of government that many believe defies measurement), he'll tell you that the secret is to keep it as simple as possible: Decide what it is you're trying to accomplish as an organization and then measure only those things that really relate to those accomplishments and that you feel fairly confident that you can influence.

Now, that's good advice and would also be a good place to end this chapter if it weren't for one other pesky word that frequently pops up around performance measurement: *benchmark*. We need to dispense with it here before it does any more damage.

The most common meaning of "benchmark" is "a search for best practices." That is, if your job in government were to keep the county highway department's trucks on the road, then your benchmarking effort would involve taking a full year and traveling the globe to find the most efficient, effective and highly praised vehicle maintenance operation in the world. And then, theoretically, you'd emulate it back home (or contract the job out to somebody who was really good at it and who would not charge you an arm and a leg).

That's straightforward enough. However, the word *benchmark* got confusing when it was co-opted as a label for an overall performance measurement program. Which is where Oregon comes in. All of the confusion surrounding the word "benchmark" is basically Oregon's fault because it named its ambitious statewide performance measurement effort "Oregon Benchmarks."

By Oregon's definition, a "benchmark" is an outcome indicator with a specific target for achievement attached. For example, one measure of how well Oregon is doing toward building the broad social well-being of its citizenry is pregnancy rates per thousand among the state's adolescent females. The state has committed itself to reducing that rate to 15 by the year 2000 (it was 19.2 in 1995). That specific target is the "benchmark" set by Oregon. (Early on, one of Oregon's benchmarks was also to have all Oregonians get at least 20 minutes of exercise three times a week, but officials quickly realized it would probably be easier to influence world peace, and so they dropped it as an indicator under the broad goal of healthy Beaver Staters.)

The problem is that other state and local performance measurers are now using the word "benchmark" in a similar fashion, so the inaccurate usage has—like a computer virus—spread nationwide. Just be ready for it.

So that's the story behind the confusion over "benchmark." Everything is perfectly clear now, right?

Well, probably not. What's important to remember is, again, that one label is not necessarily right or another necessarily wrong. The important point is that whatever you decide to call *your* performance measurement program, whether it's "that particularly stupid idea the governor is pushing this afternoon" or "the ultimate answer for all the woes of government everywhere," you need to be sure that everyone involved in your performance measurement program is on the same page when it comes to what all the terms you apply to the practice mean.

So let's take a look at how to proceed with actually implementing a performance measurement effort in your shop, because "that particularly stupid idea that the Congress/commissioner/governor/county council/mayor/department director/city manager is pushing this afternoon" is rolling your way.

Chapter 3 Quick Review
(and Jargon Cheat Sheet)

Mission: The over-arching goal of an organization boiled down to a brief statement. Let's use "promoting world peace" as our federal government example and "promoting a healthy, prosperous community" as our local government example.

Goals, outcomes or *objectives*: Slightly more specific areas of results that flow from mission. To follow our federal/local examples above: elimination of regional conflicts/healthy children community-wide.

Outcome indicators: The actual data that feed into judging progress on outcomes: Examples: number of refugees created by regional conflicts world-wide/annual rate of children who have contracted a preventable disease.

Activities: Specific actions meant to move those indicators in the right direction. Examples: sending a peace-keeping mission to the Middle East; sending a van community-wide to vaccinate children.

Outputs: Specific products meant to move those indicators in the right direction. Examples: number of peace-keeping missions deployed in a year/number of children vaccinated in a year.

Inputs: The resources mustered to create outputs. Examples: the cost of soldiers' salaries and benefits, along with the cost of equipment, transportation, bullets, guns, etc./the cost of the roving community van offering free vaccinations, nurses' salaries, the cost of vaccines, etc.

Efficiency: A look at the cost of the *inputs* that go into creating a set unit of *output*.

CHAPTER FOUR

You've Got the Ball

There are two very good reasons why governments get into performance measurement: first, to improve performance; second, to illustrate to citizens that government actually works for them. These are fine and noble goals.

But the triggering event that actually leads to the pursuit of a performance measurement plan can vary all over the lot. Perhaps your governor put together a blue-ribbon panel on government efficiency and effectiveness. It was known statewide as "the Lemon Commission," named for its chair, Bobby Joe Lemon, the state's biggest used-car dealer and a self-made millionaire (and not coincidentally, a major contributor to the governor's election campaign). The Lemon Commission, in its final report—*Soaring to New Frontiers and New Heights: Pathways to a Responsive, Responsible, Efficient, Effective and Excellent State Government into the Next Millennium and Beyond*—took the strong and revolutionary position that government needs to begin operating more like a business (but preferably not like the used-car business, which the state legislature voted to regulate a long time ago). One important step toward operating like a business, according to the report, would be to implement performance measurement. Governor Ted Passbuck agreed with the Lemon Commission and decreed that all agencies would begin doing performance measurement at once. Then they handed you the ball.

Or maybe Paul Kneejerk, chair of the state assembly's budget committee, read a fascinating article in GOVERNING magazine that discusses the difficulties in implementing performance-based budgeting. Upon finishing the article, Assemblyman Kneejerk—missing the point of the story entirely—decides that "performance-based budgeting" has a nice ring to it and figures pushing it might help him in his drive to become the state's new attorney general. And off you go.

Or perhaps the United States Congress, thinking that it is voting on a proclamation declaring August to be "Corn Appreciation Month," actually passes the Government Performance and Results Act of 1993 instead (and doesn't realize what it's done until 1997). And the next thing you know, you're having a flashback to the old Program Planning Budgeting days—only this time it's a matter of federal law.

Or maybe somebody in your government—local, state or federal—actually spent some time thinking about performance measurement and studying how it might be applied to a variety of functions within your government in order to help you do a better job. She or he then pulled together a broad-based group of staff and policy makers to investigate performance measurement's possibilities (even visiting some jurisdictions that are already trying it). Having studied the pros, cons and complications of the practice, those staffers then came up with a strategy for going ahead with a series of phased-in pilot projects in performance measurement, the ultimate goal being a rollout in all areas of government function where performance measurement makes sense. Sounds like fantasy, I know, but it *has* happened.

Anyway, for whatever reason and on whosoever's authority, here you are, ready to enter the exciting and challenging new world of results-based government...right after you untangle the latest departmental personnel crisis, and/or finish that report on the possible consolidation of field offices you were supposed to have completed a month ago, and/or brief the commissioner on upcoming testimony before Senator Bob Gasbag's Special Subcommittee on the Rising Cost of Floppy Disks in Governmental Computing, and/or read all the RFP responses on your department's new phone system...not to mention what's going on with the wife/hubby and kids at home.

STEP ONE: Lay the Groundwork

However any government decides to get into performance measurement, it is clear that two important conditions must exist in order for the effort to thrive. Now, the sad truth is that when you read what these preconditions are, you may get a little depressed. That is because they are the same two preconditions that have been listed in the hundreds of thousands of books on innovation in the public sector that preceded this one. The depressing part: There is no reason to believe that anybody is going to pay any closer attention to this discussion of the need for these preconditions than they did to the discussion in those other books. But that doesn't alter the fact that if you're in—or about to be embroiled in—a major performance measurement effort, you really need to have both.

Precondition One: inclusivity. Being at least moderately inclusive in the development of your performance measurement program is critical. In Oregon, "inclusive" meant just that. When they were launching their ambitious and now world-famous performance measurement effort, they involved just about every interest in the Beaver State. That can get a little unwieldy, and can also lead to some fairly wacky results (at one point, Oregon was actually monitoring the height-to-weight ratio of state residents, with the goal of having 91 percent of them meeting the nationally accepted guidelines by 2010). But while unwieldy, perhaps, at the end of this exercise in ultimate inclusiveness the Oregon effort had a lot of support. Now, Oregon Benchmarks has had its ups and downs, as politicians and other players have shuffled in and out, but it is surviving all the turnover, arguably because its support is truly grassroots. (See "Profiles in Implementation" at the end of this chapter for a discussion of a place at the opposite extreme, a state where the creation of the performance measurement effort included, apparently, nobody but the legislature, and which has led to some pretty wacky results, too, along with dubious longevity.)

How inclusive is inclusive? Key players should include at least those who will be directly impacted by the effort, along with those who will be called upon to support it over the long haul (in short, "customers" and "implementers").

If the initiative comes from the legislative branch, then the executive branch (including upper-level career managers) needs to be brought in, and as early as possible. If the initiative comes from the executive branch, then key legislators (including city or county councilpersons) and their staff should be included. Just as important, middle management and front-line staff need to be included, as well—not consulted, included. This is especially important in a unionized environment, since public sector employee unions tend to view every new management fad flowing their way as nothing more than the latest camouflage for "doing more with less." They pick this view up, of course, courtesy of the politician who is selling the latest management fad, not as a way to make government work better but as a way "to do more with less" (which has a much more politically appealing ring to it than "I want government to run real good"). Last, but by no means least, you need to include some representative sampling of those who actually are impacted by or who use the program or service in question. Indeed, some performance measurement gurus argue that the impactees/users (e.g., "customers") need to be consulted *first*, since your performance relates very directly to how you're serving or dealing with them.

Precondition Two: support from above. Once created, your performance effort will continue to require some upper-level support, preferably from both the legislative and the executive branch. Even if legislators are not gushing in that support, as long as they're at least not trying to kill it, a performance measurement effort can probably survive (although it may not be taken very seriously when budget time rolls around). If upper-level executive-branch officials (including, not incidentally, upper-level *career* officials) aren't on board, then the proposition is on very shaky ground. And if cabinet-level executives are resistant, then you can probably forget it, at least until more sympathetic appointees show up.

In places like Portland, Oregon; Phoenix, Arizona; and Charlotte, North Carolina, support for—or at least acceptance of—performance measurement runs from the front line, to the city manager, to the mayor's office, to the city council. And so those cities continue to make progress in building a performance base under how they do business. By contrast, the U.S. Coast Guard's GPRA-required performance measurement effort—which had strong and competent support at the highest management levels initially—was set back at least two years when a new management team decided that reorganization was more important than focusing on results. (The Coast Guard is probably the only governmental organization in the entire U.S. that actually *added* organizational layers in the past few years.)

Anyway, when it comes to laying the groundwork for a successful performance measurement effort, pray for the following: at least a modicum of high-level support; the involvement of most of those who will be impacted (including implementers and customers); some decent lead time for development and implementation, including pilot programs to clear the path and shake out the bugs; and above all, a good idea of what your government wants performance measurement to help it accomplish.

STEP TWO: Engage in a Messy and Drawn-Out Discussion About 'Mission'

Once the "go" decision has been made, the first major step in any comprehensive performance measurement effort is to establish what it is that your office, division, section, sub-section, department, agency, commission, field office, satellite bureau, directorate, duchy or whatever is supposed to be accomplishing. In many cases, this involves coming up with a mission or vision statement.

As discussed in Chapter One, vision and mission statements are touchy topics unto themselves. First of all, they very often have such a comical ring of redundancy and/or hyperbole to them that mostly you wonder what committee of self-important windbags wrote the thing: "It is the mission of the Weaselton, Tennessee, Department of Public Works to Ensure that Its Main Street Is the Finest, Smoothest, Safest, Cleanest, Most Efficiently Flowing Main Street in All of America."

But while such a mission statement might sound silly, it does do one thing: It contains the core of what the town should measure when it comes to deciding how well the DPW is doing its job. Is Main Street indeed smooth, clean and safe? Does traffic flow along it efficiently? All those are easy to quantify. "Finest" is a judgment call, but a committee of the community's most august citizenry can surely come up with some ways to measure that, whether it's judging the rich color of the blacktop or the straightness and crispness of the center lines. (As for the road's standing vis-à-vis the rest of America, they would have to compare it to other Main Streets nationwide, which any high-priced consulting firm would be happy to do for them for a small fee.)

Which is why it is probably a good idea for you take a hard swallow and try to come up with some sort of overall mission statement, however odious, redundant or foolish the job might seem. A well-crafted and straightforward mission statement serves a purpose: It will focus you on what it is you should be measuring, and it should give you a pretty good idea of how hard that will be to do. Indeed, it might tell you whether you're a candidate for performance measurement at all. Too complicated or amorphous a mission statement is an indication that you're either not very focused as an organization and/or that performance measurement won't work for you (see "All Mission Statements Mushy and Crisp" at the end of this chapter). Or it may be that you might have to modify the practice of performance measurement to fit your vague mission. By the same token, an extremely simple mission statement might indicate that a formal performance measurement effort is probably not necessary; you can eyeball your performance well enough without all the rigmarole of mission, goals and measures.

But, again, in general, mission statements are recommended. Richard Greene and Katherine Barrett, who as a journalistic team have performed admirably for years covering performance measurement in government, have a favorite example of how a mission statement can shine a spotlight on individual action, and whether that action is contributing to the greater good. It seems that pre-mission statement, the Oregon Department of Transportation had a war room where it was the job of a cadre of employees to color in maps. When asked, finally, what they were doing, the map colorers answered with that oh-so-familiar refrain that drives taxpayers oh so nuts: They were doing what they were told, they said. When asked how the coloring contributed to the organization's mission? The map colorers said they had no idea.

STEP THREE: Take a Quick Look Ahead

With a mission statement in hand, next it's probably not a bad idea to figure out what you want to accomplish in the next three, five or ten years and to plan accordingly. This is your "strategic plan." Whether or not you actually need a strategic plan depends on the scope of your responsibility and the complexity of your mission. The idea of a small municipal trash collection department having a strategic plan might strike some as a little comical; the idea of the U.S. State Department having one probably wouldn't. But it doesn't hurt to kick around the issue of what the future can or should hold in light of changing demographics, technologies, staff capacity, budgets, politics, economics and so forth, global and otherwise.

School systems, for example, are fairly notorious for waking up on any given Tuesday after Labor Day Weekend and discovering they are either 10 elementary schools short of demand or 10 over capacity. If some responsible adult were assigned the task of keeping half an eye on local birth rates and patterns of in- and out-migration, it probably wouldn't be that difficult for a school system to stay a couple of years ahead of the demand curve—which is where a strategic plan would help immensely. (The fact is, of course, that looking ahead only helps if policy makers actually *do* something with the information. Places like the city of Miami know they're following a schoolroom under-capacity curve, but they haven't actually done anything about it.)

Whether or not to come up with a strategic plan may be a decision that has already been made for you. Under GPRA, it has been: Every department in the federal government had to submit one by September 1997. In fact, under GPRA "strategic plan" includes the whole shebang: mission statement, goals/outcomes and indicators. Coming up with one that will pass congressional muster has obviously not been easy. In fact, NASA was the only federal agency that had a strategic plan approved by Congress as of the summer of 1997. Of course, they're lucky—their strategic plan is simple: to spend a lot of taxpayer money naming as many interplanetary rocks after famous cartoon characters as possible. For other agencies in the federal government, the future presents a little more complex picture.

STEP FOUR: Don't Reinvent the Wheel, the Axle, the Drive Train or the Car

OK, so you've got your mission statement, and it's powerful, flowery and inspiring. It only took about five dozen people, 135 rewrites and six months to get it. Just reading it makes you want to write your congressman in support of an anti-flag-burning amendment and put a cot in your office so you can work 24 hours a day. At the same time, you've also got your strategic plan masking-taped across the wall of the cafeteria (because you wanted to share it with all your employees; running 40 feet long as it does, it really is something to behold; plus, the plan is so brilliant, so clear and so prescient that your department is going to operate virtually on automatic pilot for the next five years, crisis-free). It probably feels to you like the battle is just about won. Of course, it hasn't been. In fact, this is where the whole process starts to get really messy.

It is at this stage of the game where many organizations start to do some serious flailing. This flailing results from the difficulty presented by choosing goals and performance measures, and the difficulty in keeping goals distinct from measures. And so this is also the stage of the performance measurement game where some outside (or perhaps even inside, if you've got an expert) help might come in handy, lest your organization spiral into a hopeless and confusing fight or wheel-spin over the mission-goals-outcomes-activities-outputs-inputs hierarchy.

Now there are good consultants out there who can help, and who are worth the money, and some governments have been very happy with the ones they've hired. There are also plenty of governments that have been badly burned by some hit-and-run artist who just changes the words in his marketing brochure to match the management fad of the day, pops in for an afternoon to do his usual song and dance and then pops out again (we'll get into this in more detail in Chapter Eight). Which is a why a good first step in this process is to ignore consultants altogether and go find another similar jurisdiction or agency that's already done all the hard work of establishing mission, goals and outcome indicators, and so forth, and borrow it. At the state and local level, the chance is 100 percent that some other department, office or agency with a similar mission (or maybe even the exact same mission) as yours has already developed a good mission-goals-outcome-activities-outputs-inputs hierarchy that you can heist and adapt.

In other words, reinventing the wheel when it comes to performance measurement is completely uncalled for. Phone or Internet around and find the place that has already done the fighting and the flailing for you. This advice holds true at the federal level, as well. While federal agencies might not be able to find an exact match as far as mission goes, there are plenty of performance measurement veterans in the federal government who can still offer some very sophisticated and real-world advice on how to begin developing good goals and realistic, helpful outcome indicators. In fact, federal officials could benefit from talking to state and local officials who've been through this and vice versa. The point is: Don't start from scratch.

With that in mind, let's cover the basic concepts of goals, outcome indicators and outputs with the understanding that (A) this discussion is meant to turn you into an educated consumer so that you can shop around for some quality outside (or inside) help; (B) that you will, in fact, shop around for some quality outside (or inside) help; and (C) that if you plan to pursue performance measurement based solely on information gleaned from this book, you will seek psychiatric counseling immediately.

Developing Goals/Outcomes

As you'll remember from Chapter Three, goals are broad categories of achievement that flow from mission. There are a couple of simple rules of thumb when it comes to developing goals. Obviously, they should have some connection to your mission. It's probably also a good idea to restrict yourself to those areas in which you believe you can have some influence, either directly or indirectly. When developing goals, aim high; don't get bogged down in detail. For example, the mission of a state environmental agency is, presumably, to protect and promote a healthy environment statewide. One goal flowing from that mission might be to protect and promote healthy wetlands. Outcome measures under that goal might include levels of algae and bacteria in the state's estuaries, levels of biodiversity in its lakes and ponds, number of auto chassis still stuck in the mud in its riparian zones, frequency of oil-slick sightings on inlets and bays, and so forth. In short, goals are a handy way to break your mission up into more tangible, bitesized pieces without being subsumed by minutia.

When developing goals, experienced practitioners argue that it is best to err on the side of identifying fewer rather than more. As a general rule of thumb, when you start getting more than about 10 or 15 goals that flow from your mission, chances are you're starting to pull in categories of accomplishment that might be tangential to your core mission—either that or you're starting to identify as "goals" areas of progress that might serve you better as "outcome indicators." For example, if you're the U.S. Environmental Protection Agency and you find yourself identifying as a "goal" cleaning up that vacant lot at the corner of PCB Avenue and Edison Boulevard in Pittsfield, Massachusetts, it's time to drift up to a higher level of abstraction, to something like: "Clean up all Superfund sites nationwide." You can let the results of specific cleanups be the measure of how well you're doing in reaching that goal.

As was mentioned earlier, it is not always necessary to duplicate the exact hierarchy of mission-goals-outcome indicators. If you are in an agency or office with a fairly specific mission, you can probably skip goals and go right to outcome indicators. For example, an animal control officer's mission is to keep the peace between mankind and creaturedom. It's probably reasonable to jump right to identifying some outcome indicators that gauge progress in meeting that mission, such as leash law compliance rates, incidences of unspayed cats on the loose, tramplings of gardens by errant moose, numbers of unlicensed squirrels in the neighborhood, vampire sightings, number of annual raccoon attacks per capita, and so forth.

On the other hand, some organizations with very complex or very broad missions sometimes develop two layers of goals before they start to list specific outcome indicators. The U.S. Department of Education's performance measurement plan, for example, has a four-tiered hierarchy: mission-goals-objectives-outcome indicators. DOE's mission: "To ensure equal access to education and to promote educational excellence throughout the nation"; one of the four goals in support of that mission: "help all students reach challenging academic standards so that they are prepared for responsible citizenship, further learning, and productive employment"; one of the seven "objectives" under that goal (in all, there are 22 objectives under the four goals): "a talented and dedicated teacher in every classroom in America"; one of the outcome indicators under that objective (there are dozens of indicators under the four goals and 22 objectives): the percentage of teachers and principals across the country who are rated by supervisors, parents and peers as "very effective." Taking a page from the Oregon performance measurement playbook, DOE's indicators are targets: they want that percentage to "increase annually" (see "To Set Targets or Not to Set Targets" on page 74).

So when developing goals, it's back to that familiar—if less-than-comforting—refrain: Go with what makes sense for your organization given what it is supposed to be accomplishing. But a simple way to think of goals is as the link between the abstract—mission—and the very specific—outcome indicators.

Those Pesky Outcome Indicators and How to Avoid the Output Trap

This is where most performance measurement efforts start to stray and stray badly. The obvious problem is that most of us are tempted to measure what's easiest to measure, or measure what we already have statistics on, whether or not any of those things really have anything to do with our list of goals or our mission. In this regard, it's particularly easy to confuse *outcome indicators* with *outputs*. For example, this chapter is already up to 3,932 words—an "output" measure. The problem is that this chapter also hasn't really done anything but confuse people, an *outcome indicator*, which gives us some idea of how the book is doing in its overall *mission* of "encouraging innovative and world-class local, state and federal government institutions that will serve citizens efficiently and effectively throughout the United States into the next millennium."

The number of citations for dogs off their leashes is an *output* measure. Incidences of dogs discovered off their leashes over a certain period of time is an *outcome indicator* that gives us some idea of how well we're doing in reaching the *mission* of ensuring that humans and creaturedom are all getting along (when dealing with such a straightforward task as animal control, as you'll recall, we decided it's safe to skip the *goal* layer of the program and go right from mission to outcome indicator).

The number of speeding tickets issued is an *output* measure; the number of auto accidents due to speeding is an *outcome indicator* that gives us some idea of the progress we're making toward our *goal* of a safe driving environment, which feeds into our *mission* of "ensuring safe communities."

And if we were to adopt the U.S. Department of Education's four-tiered performance measurement hierarchy, it would go something like: Percentage of teachers who've taken their recertification tests is an *output* measure, while the percentage who scored well on those tests is an *outcome indicator* that gives us some idea of how we're doing toward our *objective* of good teachers in every classroom, which feeds into our *goal* of students ready to be good workers and citizens, which flows from our *mission* of ensuring equal access to excellent education for all, and so forth. Again (and prob-

To Set Targets or Not to Set Targets

One debate among performance measurement practitioners is whether or not to set specific performance targets. Some believe that setting targets keeps an organization focused and energized; others argue that such an exercise can be politically perilous (it's embarrassing to miss the targets, on the one hand; it might cost you your job, on the other). The goal of performance measurement, argue those in the latter group, should be to develop a baseline for performance and then strive for continuous improvement.

There is ample anecdotal evidence that setting targets is a good way to spur performance, though. For example, in 1988, the U.S. EPA launched what it called its "33/50" program, the aim of which was to work with industry in voluntarily reducing the release of high-priority toxic chemical waste a full 50 percent by 1995, with an interim goal of 33 percent by 1992. Both targets were achieved, even before the deadlines.

On the other hand, setting—and then missing—targets *does* have the potential to be embarrassing. Oregon,

ably ad nauseum) *outputs* are some product of government activity; *outcome indicators* are the real gauge of how we're doing by way of results.

The problem is that many governments don't really make (or understand) the distinction. Indeed, many governments start to quickly veer off of the performance measurement path by simply measuring what is handy, whether such information is relevant to results or not, and what's handy is usually numbers on outputs. This, apparently, is an especially major problem in areas of regulation and law enforcement, because lots of regulatory and law for example, vowed in 1992 that by 1995 it would move from Number 6 to Number 1 in *Financial World* magazine's ranking of well-run states. In 1995, however, Oregon weighed in at Number 25, "a gentle reminder," notes Richard Kirk Jonas, deputy director of Virginia's Joint Legislative Audit and Review Commission, "that ambitious goals are easier to set than to achieve."

In a paper on applying performance measurement to environmental programs, Shelley Metzenbaum, formerly with the U.S. EPA and now director of the Performance Measurement Project at the Kennedy School of Government, argues that goal-setting, working against an internal baseline and comparing your performance with somebody else's are all good motivators, and that any effective performance measurement effort should probably include all three of those. She is probably right.

Setting targets is certainly very scary, though, particularly for government employees who are used to getting blamed when things don't go as planned. On the other hand, it can be, as stated earlier, an effective motivator. Ultimately, whether setting targets is viewed as energizing or merely as a setup will always boil down to how "results" are used: to improve or to punish.

enforcement agencies are off the path.

For example, a police department might be racking up very impressive numbers of arrests and presenting those numbers as evidence of departmental effectiveness. But clearly those numbers only mean something as they relate to crime rates (and, ultimately, to how safe citizens feel). Regulatory agencies, likewise, have a tendency to confuse outputs and outcome indicators. Again, a regulatory agency could be papering the world with tough citations while ignoring the issue of whether those citations are actually helping the agency accomplish its mission, whether that mission is the fair and efficient collection of taxes or to keep workers safe and healthy.

Reasonable, Intelligent People Finally Spring to Action

Now, reasonable, intelligent people might wonder how it is that reasonable, intelligent people could consider something like the number of speeding tickets issued in a week as a relevant measure of bottom-line results—whether or not you've got a safe driving environment. Well, it happens all the time (remember the good old IRS and its good old quota system?), and it brings us to the strange case of the Federal Occupational Safety and Health Administration.

Sometime around 1991, somebody was thumbing through state-by-state OSHA statistics when he noticed something weird. The state of Maine finished in the top five of all states in two attention-getting ways: It finished high in number of citations written (indicating that in Maine the regulators were out there banging heads and slapping wrists like there was no tomorrow). And it also finished high in the whole area of per-capita rates of death and injury among workers.

That led to a sort of obvious question: How could that be? How could a state where OSHA is holding a veritable annual ticker tape parade with citations also be one of the most dangerous in which to work?

The answer: The OSHA citations being written in Maine bore little relationship to where the mayhem and destruction were actually occurring among Maine's workers. The problem is that the state's OSHA regulators had been so focused on cranking out those citations (good productivity) that nobody was asking whether there was any correlation between who was getting cited in Maine and where and how people were actually getting hurt and killed.

And so Maine and OSHA got together to do the logical thing: talk about real performance. Pretty quickly they figured out that using the intensity of the blizzard caused by flying citations to gauge performance was—to use a term of public management art—not too smart. Better, they figured, to focus on a new area of performance: actually improving worker safety.

The new plan: Inspectors started to focus on those industries and occupations where the most workers were getting banged up. Along with that, and also in the spirit of improved performance, regulators started working cooperatively with the regulated community, as well, developing ways to make workplaces and jobs safer. The results were impressive and predictable: In just two years, Maine workers' injury and illness claims fell by more than one-third.

(The U.S. Department of Transportation is trying something slightly similar in its truck-safety enforcement program. Rather than pound on every trucking company equally, the DOT is now gathering data on which companies have good safety records and which don't. The plan is to focus on those companies with poor records.)

So as you proceed with this whole performance measurement exercise, it is very important that you keep your eyes on the prize and not on that file cabinet over there stuffed with tons of numbers you can get your hands on real fast, as tempting as that might be, because they're probably not numbers that really tell you anything about performance.

If in Doubt, Ask

Besides, it's not always numbers that allow you to vector in on performance, which brings us to two other types of outcome indicators that those who are good at all this turn to when trying to gauge how well government is doing in achieving some public objective or other: the observations of "trained observers" and "customer/citizen surveys."

Trained observers are used when looking around is the best way to objectively assess a government's performance in some area or other. For example, trained observers are used to judge the effectiveness of municipal street-cleaning operations. Trained observers eyeball a sampling of streets and back alleys, and they assign each thoroughfare a numerical rating for cleanliness. (Portland, Maine, even has trained sniffers, who respond to citizen complaints about olfactory insults.)

Customer and citizen surveys are, likewise, used when other data can't tell the whole story. A government may be efficient in issuing driver's licenses, for example, but that doesn't mean that citizens necessarily feel well treated down at the old DMV. And so in some agencies that serve the public, citizen/customers are asked to fill out questionnaires rating the service they received while visiting a particular arm of government. Even more broadly, citizen surveys are increasingly being used to get some sense of how government is doing in achieving larger societal goals (larger, even, than whether the last trip to the DMV was a Nordstrom's Experience).

One of the typical areas for such a survey of the citizenry is public safety. It's relatively easy to gin up good outcome indicators on such things as case-closing rates, rates of muggings, rates of car thefts, and so forth, but that doesn't tell you how your police department is doing in its broader mission of building a general sense among citizens that they live in a safe place. Nor does it tell you how well-served citizens feel by their police department. And so in many places, governments ask such questions as "Do you feel safe?" or "Was your last interaction with a police officer a satisfying one?" In fact, many local governments now send out a general citizen satisfaction survey by which they gauge the general state of the citizens' mood in a host of areas related to government activity and service, not just public safety. (Prince William County, Virginia, publishes a very good one that is worth getting a copy of. For information on how to do that, see "If You're Still Serious..." at the end of this book.)

Finally, the customer satisfaction survey is also being more frequently used to gauge the quality of internal governmental operations. For example, one of the most important (and frequently vilified) administrative support systems in government is its personnel office. And so enlightened personnel offices are starting to ask other agencies to rate how the personnel department is doing in fulfilling its mission of helping find good people and get them hired into government jobs. (Some say that if Georgia's personnel system had done this years ago, then the state legislature wouldn't have voted to sunset it, which it did about two years ago with the whole-hearted support and applause of other department directors statewide.)

Two things make such surveys more practical these days: The science of surveying has improved considerably, and they've gotten less expensive to do as governments have learned how to tap local universities and other lower-cost and nearby resources for help in conducting them. Prince William County, for example, gets help from the University of Virginia in doing its county-wide citizen survey. At the same time, there are resources such as Hatry's *Customer Surveys for Agency Managers*, mentioned in Chapter One on page 27.

Results on Time

In any event, whatever the outcome indicator you choose—whether hard statistics, the observations of air-sniffers or the results of citizen-satisfaction surveys—they have to be one other thing besides relevant to results: They must be timely, too.

Timely reporting is important for a simple reason: Ideally, the outcome indicators a government chooses offer a close-to-immediate chance to judge whether some action is impacting some outcome indicator and, therefore, progress toward some policy goal. Police have boosted patrols in a certain neighborhood where drug activity has been reported. The number of drug-related incidents in that neighborhood is down in the wake of the new patrol schedule, and citizens in that neighborhood are responding on a 94 percent basis that they feel it's OK to go out at night. If all that data rolls in in a timely fashion, then policy makers are able to confidently make a connection between the more aggressive, targeted patrolling and a satisfied citizenry.

For example, New York Mayor Rudolph Giuliani started pushing his police officers in 1997 to aggressively enforce both traffic and pedestrian laws. He did this for a simple reason: New York pedestrians and bicyclists had been getting mowed down by cars, trucks and buses in amazing numbers every year. The push wasn't popular, though, particularly among pedestrians, who consider jaywalking in New York City to be a constitutional right. But data from the first half of 1998 show something interesting: 71 pedestrians and bicyclists were killed in that six-month period, compared with 111 in the same period in 1997, before the mayor's enforcement push took hold.

To the outside observer, 71 probably still seems like quite a high casualty rate, but as anybody who has ever been to New York City can attest, it's a drop in the bucket when it comes to the numbers of drivers, pedestrians and cyclists competing for the right of way in the Big Apple on any given street over the course of any given day. Back to the point: Having such timely statistics has allowed the city to claim with quite a bit of credibility that its safety campaign is working. Not incidentally, it has also served to quiet down critics of the stepped-up enforcement, and fast.

But Eagles Weren't Saved in a Day

There are times, though, when the results of some government action won't show up for a long time, maybe even years. In 1972, the U.S. EPA banned the use of the pesticide DDT on the well-substantiated theory that it was interfering with the reproduction of many kinds of birds. Yet it wasn't until decades after the ban that the policy achieved one of its major goals: the recovery of the bald eagle population. The question, then, is: What do you measure in the meantime that offers you some interim gauge of progress?

For those government activities that might not have immediate and obvious impacts, performance measurement gurus have come up with a performance marker known as an "interim measure," also sometimes called a "surrogate measure." A logical interim measure (or *interim outcome indicator*, to offer up a mouthful) in the case above would be evidence of a drastic reduction in the use of DDT nationwide. In fact, the environment is an obvious area where interim measures come in handy, because environmental cleanup is often a very long-term proposition. The U.S. can measure the extent to which it has slowed the growth in emission of greenhouse gases (an interim outcome indicator). But it will probably be quite a while before it can tell with any certainty that slowing that growth is having the intended impact of slowing or stopping global warming (a more down-the-road indicator in assessing progress toward the goal of improved global environmental health).

Some Indicator Is Better than None at All, but None at All Is Better than a Bad One

There are times—particularly early on in a performance measurement effort—when you have neither interim nor ultimate outcome indicators; output measures are all you've got, because that's all you've been collecting data on. For example, you have file folders full of data on how many speeding tickets you've issued, but you have no centralized information on how many traffic accidents you had last year that were directly attributable to people driving too fast. And so for the time being, you're going to sub in ticket-writing as an outcome indicator, knowing that it is inadequate in figuring out how you're doing in achieving the goal of safer driving conditions for all. That's fine, as long as you understand that in doing so you are not measuring real results, and as long as you begin to gather data on real results as soon as practicable.

But when you do go ahead and choose that outcome indicator, pick the right one. As Richard Kirk Jonas, deputy director of Virginia's Joint Legislative Audit and Review Commission, points out in a case study he wrote on Virginia's performance measurement effort, it is important to consider very carefully whether the indicator you choose actually captures real information on performance. "A bad performance measure can be worse than no performance measure at all," argues Jonas. (For information on how to get Jonas's case study, see the reference to the American Society for Public Administration in "If You're Still Serious..." at the end of this book.)

Jonas's favorite example comes courtesy of the U.S. Army, which back in the 1970s was worried about unit morale (it's hard to believe there was a morale problem back then, with the war in Vietnam going so swimmingly well) and was knocking around for ways to measure it. One measure the brass chose was absent-without-leave rates, on the plausible theory that a unit with lots of soldiers who were chronically AWOL wasn't a happy one. The problem is that commanders—afraid they'd be criticized for high AWOL rates—simply changed the definition of AWOL from being absent even a few minutes after midnight to missing morning formation. In other words, soldiers who wanted to stay out all night were given the green light, which, Jonas argues, didn't help performance or morale at all. Now, some soldiers might argue that morale actually improved considerably in the wake of the new policy, and maybe it did. But the point is, AWOL rates are no way to measure any of that. In fact, unit morale would probably have been gauged much more accurately by simply asking soldiers how they felt about things. So when choosing outcome indicators, think hard about whether they really measure what you want to measure and whether the decision to measure a certain thing might not have some unintended consequence.

Which segues into a final point about embarking on a performance measurement effort: You're never done. As you develop measures and try to apply them, you'll find that some work and some don't. Some have unintended consequences that you might not like; some might just miss the mark; you may learn that with some you really don't have much control over outcomes; some might just need to be tweaked; or you may need new ones as the mission of your organization evolves. At any rate, the refinement process should be ongoing. "We go through all of our measures every year. You have to to make sure they're not stale and that they're still capturing the information you need," says Herb Hill, with the Virginia Department of Planning and Budget.

STEP FIVE: Look Up the Hall, Down the Hall and in the Mirror

With these basics under your belt, you've got a decision to make: Is performance measurement something that will actually help you do your job better, or will it just be a distracting time-waster? If you decide it will help—or if that decision has already been made for you whether it makes sense or not, whether you like it or not, and whether you have the support of top levels of management or not—then the best thing to do is quit stalling and get rolling. As suggested under Step Four, find someone who can give you some good, common-sense and targeted advice on how to proceed, and start making some decisions about mission, goals and outcome indicators, even if it means having to go back and refine and rejigger later.

Now, there are those who, having looked squarely in the mirror, will swear that performance measurement can't possibly be applied to as complex a job as theirs. To those valiant legions, we dedicate the next chapter: "Measuring the Unmeasurable." You're not going to like it.

Before you skip to that chapter, however, it is important to repeat the admonition from the Introduction of the book that performance measurement is not an exact science. How you apply performance measures to what you do will depend on a host of circumstances. And, chances are, your attempts at implementation will, like most others, be fraught with conflict and untold messiness. Anyone who has been involved in setting up a comprehensive performance measurement program will tell you unequivocally how hard it is. "It's like giving birth," says Martha Marshall, who helped, and continues to help, Prince William County implement its performance measurement plan. And when Marshall says "It's like giving birth," she doesn't mean that warm, fuzzy, baby-wrapped-in-a-blanket-and-gurgling-quietly-and-contentedly-in-its-mother's-arms part of the birth. She means the part just before that.

Chapter 4 Quick Quiz

1. An indication that your performance measurement effort is adequately inclusive might be:

    a. you're polling street people as part of developing your DPW's performance measurement plan.

    b. at the last meeting, somebody started singing "We Are the World."

    c. you understand the difference between "inside" and "outside" customers, and each is represented in your planning group.

2. One indication that your performance measurement effort has good upper-level support is:

    a. your immediate supervisor seems to have glued her door shut.

    b. the mayor has decided that his wife's psychic has some good ideas about improving government performance that he'd like you to hear about.

    c. you were actually asked by your boss to brief a group of other department heads about progress in developing *your* department's strategic plan.

3. A *mission* of a state personnel department might be:

    a. to make every other department head in state government crazy.

b. to test where no man has tested before.

c. to ensure that state government is manned (and womanned) by the best.

4. A good way to evaluate which of the *goals* you've chosen are worth keeping would be:

a. tack a bunch of them to the wall and get out the darts.

b. use them all.

c. ask those whom you are supposed to serve, support or assist to take a look at them and be the judge.

5. A good *outcome indicator* for your Department of Code Enforcement would be:

a. amount of cash and in-kind bribes received by inspectors in the last quarter.

b. number of citations issued in the last quarter.

c. rates of compliance with building codes on first inspections in the last quarter.

All Mission Statements Mushy and Crisp

Here are the mission statements of the U.S. Commerce Department and the U.S. Coast Guard. You can decide for yourself which organization is more focused.

Mission Statement of the U.S. Department of Commerce

The Department of Commerce promotes job creation, economic growth, sustainable development, and improved living standards for all Americans, by working in partnership with business, universities communities, and workers to:

1. Build for the future and promote U.S. competitiveness in the global marketplace by strengthening and safeguarding the nation's economic infrastructure;

2. Keep America competitive with cutting-edge science and technology and an unrivaled information base; and,

3. Provide effective management and stewardship of our nation's resources and assets to ensure sustainable economic opportunities.

Mission Statement of the U.S. Coast Guard:

Our mission is to protect the public, the environment, and U.S. economic interests through the prevention and mitigation of marine incidents.

Profiles in Implementation; Or the United States Congress as Unlikely and Then Predictable Role Model

A responsible book author would start this essay with a detailed description of a government that has gone about developing and implementing its performance measurement effort the right way. But that wouldn't be as much fun as diving right into a description of a government that did it the dumb way, so let's do the dumb way first.

A dumb way to go about implementing performance measurement would be to do what South Carolina did recently, which was for the legislature to pass a law requiring that its whole higher education system be on a 100 percent performance-based *budget* footing by the year 1999.

This one is a little bit of a head-scratcher. Granted, the South Carolina legislature didn't have access to the brilliant discussion of performance measurement contained in these pages before forging ahead with such a quarter-baked idea. Which is why legislators probably fell back on that good rock-ribbed conservative, private-sector, no-nonsense, kick 'em-in-the-pants approach to public management: Somebody, anybody needs to be held accountable for results. And in this case, those who needed to be held accountable were those pointy-headed, ivy-smoking, tenured academics and their spendthrift administrative handlers.

The problem that you get into rather quickly,

however, is: accountable for what results? It's one thing if you're talking about the Department of Public Works in the (made-up) town of Weaselton, Tennessee, population 105. The DPW is responsible for keeping one road in good shape, and everybody in town knows whether Hank and his boys are getting the job done. (One thing they do wonder about is why it takes 14 men and eight town trucks to do it; see the discussion of "efficiency" in Chapter Six.)

It's another thing if you're the (not made-up) South Carolina higher education system. Do you measure success by how well graduates score on standardized tests? Or maybe success is measured by attendance, attrition and graduation rates. Some might argue that the success of the system is measured by the number of students who go on to satisfying careers. Or maybe success should really be measured by the number of truly deep-thinking—if unemployable—philosophy majors that the system deposits into the cruel, real world each year.

The fact is, there are many possible measures of success of a state's university and college system, and all that is worth discussing. But the likelihood that 100 percent of a state higher ed system's budget can be pegged to performance is plain silly. Such a decree merely serves to underscore the naivete of the legislature about what performance measurement is and what it can do.

Legislators, undoubtedly, would have been well served by at least consulting with educational experts (hey, maybe even some of the folks in their own state's higher ed system) before coming up with this legislative clunker.

SO WHAT'S THE BETTER WAY? In Minnesota, the legislature teamed up with the executive branch to pass its 1993 performance measurement law, which requires that all major state agencies publish annual performance reports. While the law didn't give those agencies a whole lot of time before the first reports were due (only a year, in fact), there was no explicit penalty for agency wheel-spinning, and there was certainly no pie-in-the-sky effort to start pegging 100 percent of any agency's budget to performance within a couple of years. The idea was to get the legislature and executive-branch agencies comfortable and familiar with the whole concept of performance measurement first.

And that was a smart way to proceed with a performance measurement effort, especially in light of the fact that the effort in Minnesota hasn't experienced totally smooth sailing. According to an American Society for Public Administration report on Minnesota's performance measurement effort: "In general, [Minnesota's agency] performance reports have proven to be more difficult, costly, and time-consuming than legislators or agency officials expected." That's not much of a revelation; this stuff is hard to do.

What *is* startling about what's going on in Minnesota is that the executive branch and the legislature are actually working with each other on it. Just finding the words "legislators" and "agency officials" in the same sentence (and so close together) in the ASPA report indicates that Minnesota is on the right track. Indeed, responsibility for rollout and overview of the state's performance measurement effort is jointly held by the Minnesota Department of Finance and the Legislative Auditor's office. And while it has been a struggle in Minnesota, the state has scored some early and significant breakthroughs.

For example, as part of its own performance measurement plan (and under the heading of "physician, heal thyself"), the Minnesota Department of Finance has moved away from calculating the *number* of fiscal forecasts it produces each year as a measure of its effectiveness, and toward—get ready for a shocker—*assessing the accuracy of those forecasts!* An excellent example of a governmental entity shifting from measuring out*puts* to out*comes*.

THERE IS AT LEAST ONE other governmental entity that actually approached implementation of performance measurement in a semi-sensible way, and that is—speaking of shockers—the U.S. Congress. The one thing it did right in passing GPRA in 1993 was to include a fairly long-term and staggered phase-in. The law even called for volunteers to pilot performance measurement before it was to become mandatory. And so those departments that took GPRA seriously were able to get started with the reasonable hope of meeting GPRA's down-the-road deadlines.

That's about all Congress did right, however. Among the many things that Congress did wrong in passing GPRA was that it failed to calculate the sheer size and complexity of the enterprise, which is why such titles as *The Government Performance and Results Act; Governmentwide Implementation Will Be Uneven* appear on U.S. Government Accounting Office reports on GPRA implementation ("uneven" being one of those words that report writers use when "stinko" would be politically unacceptable). Nor did Congress develop any ongoing strategy for communicating to the executive branch that it was serious about implementation (assuming that it *was* serious way back then). Nor did Congress set up any special clearinghouse for helping departments implement GPRA; rather, it heaped that job onto the Office of Management and Budget, which actually already had plenty to do, thanks. Nor has Congress outlined what it plans to do to laggard agencies that don't meet the GPRA deadlines; will it help them, or punish them, or—as many expect—just ignore them? And so on and so forth. Then again, one should not lay total blame on such a busy institution as the United States Congress for its failure to follow through. After all, they have bigger fish to fry, such as trying to decide whether "National Potbelly Pig Appreciation Week" should last five days or seven.

CHAPTER FIVE

Measuring the Unmeasurable

ere's an exercise to do during lunch today: Sit at your desk and write down a list of everything that government—local, state and federal—does. Don't let any grease from your hamburger drip on the piece of paper.

OK, now look at your list. You'll notice that it's long...in fact, you got so absorbed by this fascinating exercise that it's now 5 p.m. and time to go home.

You'll also notice there are some general categories of governmental activity that would seem to defy performance measurement for one reason or another. In some cases, it may be tough to get people to agree on outcomes. Or it may be that coming up with outcomes is easy, but trying to establish cause and effect is almost impossible. Or sometimes the results of some governmental actions may not show up for so long that it seems almost ridiculous to try to measure the results. Or maybe it's a type of work the results of which just can't be measured.

The snap conclusion you might come to is that there are those agencies or departments in government that simply aren't well suited to performance measurement and never will be, barring some amazing alignment of consensus on mission, or barring development of some magical technology that all of a sudden allows tracking the untrackable or establishing cause and effect when none seemed to exist previously.

And if you happen to believe that you work in one of those agencies, your response may be understandable. You file the latest performance measurement directive beneath the nearest flowerpot, where it could perform the important function of absorbing the overflow from twice-weekly waterings.

But as explained in Chapter Two, you're probably not going to get away with that tactic for very long, because lots of people are out there busily figuring out how to apply performance measures to some areas heretofore considered immune, such areas as social services, higher education, economic development and even the toughest nut of all, international relations.

Outcomes and Humankind

When the whole idea of performance measurement was resurfacing in the public sector in earnest in the early 1990s, it was in the area of social services that folks were quickest to dismiss the possibility that it could ever be applied.

The social services world had good reasons for the stance: The mission of a social services department is diffuse, encompassing helping everyone from the unemployed to the insane. Plus, the feds, state governments, local governments, for-profit and not-for-profit service providers, hospitals, charities, families and so forth all have a piece of the action. On top of that, trying to establish cause and effect in a field so tied to the vagaries and frailties of humankind just didn't seem very fair...or enlightened. Furthermore, national, state and local economic factors could have as much impact on the "performance" of a social services agency as the quality or quantity of services offered. Kick-start the economy of a depressed rural county with an auto factory or two, and you'll be amazed at what the county social services department will begin to accomplish in the way of lowered welfare rolls and reduced spouse abuse.

Of course, outside factors always influence everything. A sophisticated performance measurement program doesn't claim to illustrate seamless cause and effect when seamless cause and effect doesn't exist. A sophisticated performance measurement program acknowledges that there are influences and issues beyond one's control, and/or that achieving progress in some area might involve the work of other governmental or non-governmental partners. Which is why in the whole social services area, those who believe in tracking performance aren't necessarily hewing to anything like the old physics dictum: For every action there is an equal and opposite reaction. When Brian Wing, commissioner of the Office of Temporary and Disability Assistance for New York State, was implementing performance measurement in his shop, he flatly stated that certain upstate counties in New York were chronic laggards in the department's 35-county quarterly performance reports. The reason wasn't necessarily that those counties were run by incompetents; in many cases it was in large part due to a continuing shaky upstate economy.

But Wing doesn't believe that's much of a reason not to measure performance. If you're tracking data—such as how many people are coming on and going off welfare on a county-by-county basis—it at least allows you ask good, targeted questions about what's going on in a particular place or with a particular program. It may indeed turn out that a county social services department is performing to the best of its abilities and that forces beyond the department's control are heavily influencing results. On the other hand, it may be that the department really isn't doing a very good job. Either way, those are good things to know so that officials can fashion a sensible response—even if that response sometimes might be to do very little.

Toward that end, New York State now releases county-by-county performance reports on how it is doing in various areas of social services and social services delivery, including such measures as "percent of TANF cases closed due to earnings," or "number of abuse/maltreatment reports received per 1,000 children under age 18" over a certain period of time, or "median length of stay in foster care for all children in foster care" as of a specific date, or "percent of out-of-wedlock children with paternity established" as of a certain date.

But rather than just release the data in some raw form, Wing decided to do one other controversial thing: He decided to rank counties by performance. Some counties don't like it, arguing that it's not fair, that there *are* frequently forces beyond a county social service department's control that impact performance. But state officials like Wing aren't very sympathetic. He agrees that it may not always be fair—and he allows counties to include explanatory narratives along with the raw data they submit—but he asserts that the comparisons stir up lively and valuable discussion, not only about things like the performance of caseworkers in a certain county but also about different tactics that the various counties use to accomplish certain tasks, such as establishing paternity. A top performer might have something to teach a county at the back of the pack.

And the rankings *do* also lead to discussion of external issues, such as the overall strength of the state's economy and what government can or can't do about that. Again, that discussion may turn to forces over which a social services agency has no control, such as the relative success of state or local economic development programs. But that can be helpful, too, drawing in other officials in other parts of government to consider outside issues that might be impacting the social services picture in the state.

Cause and effect aside, Wing finds that the comparisons

help for one other simple reason: Knowing that they'll be publicly ranked against their peers *does* spur counties to higher levels of performance. It's just human nature.

Now, lots of people will wonder why New York gets highlighted here, inasmuch as it is just one state out of many that are now applying performance measures to social services and its system is by no means perfect (neither the technology nor the methodology is there yet). Nor is its performance measurement system the most advanced, when compared with other states, such as Virginia, Washington and Iowa. What's interesting about the Empire State is that, as famous as it is for its bloated and wheezy bureaucracies and its staggeringly large social service caseloads, it is still going ahead and putting a performance footing under how it now does business, and it *is* making good progress. And if New York can do it, few other states have much excuse for not trying it themselves.

Given that a number of states are further along, it's certainly worth looking at at least one, just to get some idea of how detailed and ambitious some of these performance measurement efforts—again in areas once regarded as impossible to measure—have become.

In Iowa, the state established a Council on Human Investment to help develop what Iowa calls "state policy objectives" in virtually every area of government tended to by the executive branch. In establishing those policy objectives (and ways to measure progress toward them), the state hasn't been shy about applying the practice to social services. Two objectives, for example, focus on two of the toughest-to-achieve results of social service programs: reduced alcohol and drug abuse, on the one hand, and improved self-sufficiency, on the other.

Under reducing drug and alcohol abuse, specific outcome indicators include rates of alcohol-related car crashes and rates of drug use among youth. Self-sufficiency indicators include the average length of time spent on public assistance, the proportion of families at any given time that need assistance, the proportion of parents paying child support, and the proportion of kids living in poverty.

As data under each of these indicators build, Iowa, obviously, is going to have a pretty good idea whether the social services programs (outputs) it has designed and implemented are actually working.

But measuring the effect of social services programs isn't only allowing governments to evaluate their own programs. As we'll see in Chapter Nine, developing good performance measures in the social services arena has allowed governments to more accurately assess the performance of contractors. Some jurisdictions are now even writing performance-based contracts for social service agencies, making payments to contract service providers contingent on measurable outcomes (as opposed to the good old-fashioned use of outputs, i.e., number of clients seen, or placed in a job training or drug rehab programs, or hours put in by caseworkers, and so forth). In fact, in some places, the deal is now a simple one: no results, no cash.

Applying Outcome Measures to Higher Ed; Or Five Years and $50,000 Later...

People love to argue about the quality of the education that Americans get, and how as a nation we're becoming a collection of pretty dim bulbs. The headlines in this regard are always dire: A January 5, 1997, article from *The New York Times* is typical: "Learning Gap Tied to Time In the System; As School Stay Grows, Scores on Tests Worsen." Now that's when you know you're really achieving something as an educational system.

There are, of course, lots of ways to evaluate the relative brain power of your average American, but the typical way is the good old general-knowledge quiz, one that has real relevance to day-to-day life. And so we're asked to locate the Congo River on a world map, to recite the "Tomorrow and

Tomorrow and Tomorrow" soliloquy from *Macbeth* by heart, explain what a regression equation is and when one might be used, and to identify the sentence from which the participle is dangling. So far, roving inquisitors have been able to find few Americans who can do any of the four, never mind all of them.

Such dubious outcome indicators notwithstanding, there are actually well-accepted types of tests for establishing how bright we actually are or aren't, at least early on in life. There is a boatload of tests keeping entire testing industries afloat that measure how smart pre-schoolers are, or how ready a junior high school student is for high school, or how ready a high school student is for college.

We still like to argue about educational testing, and the whole debate over national standards and testing has reached a hysterical pitch, but the fact is that when it comes to gauging the relative smarts of teens and pre-teens, we've pretty much got the drill down. (For an excellent example at the state level, it is worth looking at Texas's Assessment of Academic Skills tests for grades 1-12. Not only is the testing solid, but the state is able to disaggregate results in a way that allows officials to really home in on trouble spots.)

A trickier nut to crack is evaluating higher education. As discussed in Chapter Four, who's to say what the real goal or outcome of a college or postgraduate education is? There are those of us, after all, who upon trying to engage a typical public administration doctoral student in anything resembling substantive discussion recall that alarming January 5, 1997, *Times* headline.

But again, that hasn't kept people from trying to come up with some set of measures to apply so that we might begin to get some handle on the basics. Indeed, an entire research institution has been developed to study the issue: the Center for Effective Public Higher Education at the Rockefeller Institute of Government in Albany, New York. According to the center's director, Joseph C. Burke, about 10 states are looking at establishing performance measures in their public higher education systems.

Here's what the states are typically trying to measure: enrollment and graduation rates; time to degree (remember your freshman-year roommate, the funny plants he grew on your windowsill, and the good old seven-year plan?); pass rates on professional exams; job placement rates; data on graduates' satisfaction with their jobs; and faculty workload and productivity as measured by student/teacher ratios, along with hours spent (actually) teaching.

Now, the astute reader will immediately notice that what states are measuring mostly looks like out*puts*, not out*comes*. Enrollment and graduation rates, faculty workload and productivity measures, along with data on time to degree, don't tell us much about outcomes, if we agree that outcomes should focus more on a graduate's ultimate future success in life. Which is why states begin to nose into results territory when they look at pass rates on professional exams (law boards, medical boards and the like, which measure knowledge, if not ethics or bedside manner), along with such things as job placement and job satisfaction.

Clearly, when it comes to measuring performance, the brave pioneers who are trying to apply it to higher education aren't there yet, if they're ever going to get there. But they're at least giving it a shot. And if they stick with it, they will get better at it. And let's face it, now that you've got two kids about to enter college, you probably at least want to know that 80 percent of students enrolled at Big State U. actually escape with bachelor's degrees within a reasonable amount of time—say, under $50,000-worth of time—even if you'll still have no idea whether they're any smarter for the spending.

Taking the 'Con' Out of Economic Development

States, localities and the feds spend billions of dollars a year on economic development programs, from business recruitment to foreign trade missions to job-training programs to tourism. As of this writing—with the U.S. economy bouncing along like a teenager on a six-pack of triple-caffeinated Blast Cola—those investments all seem to have paid off. Of course, 25 years hence (at which time this book will have taken its rightful place as one of the classic texts in public administration), when we're trying to finance a three-front war with Canada, France and Freedonia over control of iron ore mines on Mars, it might be a different economic story. But at this moment, the aforementioned investments have arguably done the trick. Unemployment is at record lows; profits are soaring; Wall Street is bubbling (well, it *was*); consumers are spending; city, state and federal coffers are bulging. The future seems bright. So government should be taking a lot of credit here, right?

The problem is that measuring the impact of economic development programs just seems way too tentative a proposition. After all, the forces that impact economic performance are unpredictable, ranging from the weather to the latest international (or domestic) political crisis, to what the chairman of the Federal Reserve happened to say to his five-year-old over breakfast that morning.

And maybe that's the place to leave it, except that in spending billions of dollars on economic development, governments would seem to be explicitly acknowledging that they *do* have some influence over their own economic well-being. Otherwise, why all the spending? And so the question stands: How much influence do they have?

It's a question that governments don't seem too eager to answer, actually. If they were, then Harry Hatry would have sold more copies of the book he co-authored, *Monitoring the Outcomes of Economic Development Programs*, another in the series of good technical manuals on public sector performance measurement published by the Urban Institute. In fact, instead of being down to his very last copy of the book, Hatry's got a basement full of them. It seems that governments aren't doing a whole lot of outcome measurement in this area, even though lots of people frequently ask where economic and community development dollars are going, and to what effect.

Now, it is not the purpose of this chapter to argue that governments *should* be trying to measure the impact of their economic development programs. It is merely the purpose of this chapter to illustrate that even in areas regarded as defying measurement—such as economic development—somebody has come up with a methodology for at least trying.

Hatry's book is broken down into six sections of activity. They are (*this* author's interpretations of categories added in parentheses):

1. business attraction ("tax giveaway-based smokestack chasing")
2. assistance to existing businesses ("undercutting the giveaway tax-incentive package that rival Ohio just offered to one of your major upstate manufacturers")
3. financial assistance ("slush")
4. tourism promotion ("You've got a friend in Poughkeepsie!")
5. export promotion ("junketeering"), and
6. community economic development assistance ("pork")

Getting a copy of Hatry's book would be a good first step for governments that want to delete the parentheticals above. Again, few seem interested in doing that, which does make you wonder about how effective all those economic development programs really are. But if government officials want to start trying to measure their performance, a good guide exists to help them start trying, and here are some of the ways how: Under "business attraction and marketing programs," for example, the effect of a given jurisdiction's economic development strategies might be judged in three basic areas: "service quality," "intermediate outcomes" and "long-term outcomes." Service quality can be measured by asking businesses that have contacted your economic development office how responsive the office was. Intermediate outcomes might include the number of companies that, after initial contact with the economic development office, actually came and visited the jurisdiction. Long-term outcomes might include the number of such firms that ultimately made the move, the amount of capital investment they made in your jurisdiction, the jobs they added, the number of fast-food joints that sprang up on the roads to their plants, and so forth.

Again, the methodology isn't leakproof, but it at least gives governments a general idea of whether or not what they're doing in a particular area makes much of a difference.

Measuring Diplomacy

For those in government who really don't want to try to measure the impact of what they do—and who steadfastly argue that it's impossible to measure what they do—Ambassador Craig Johnstone presents a problem. That is because as head of policy and planning at the U.S. State Department, Johnstone is trying to apply performance measurement in the one area that arguably resists it above any other: international relations. If the result of any area of governmental activity is tough to quantify or is impacted by myriad forces beyond anyone's control, after all, it's foreign affairs. Yet even if the Government Performance and Results Act had never passed, Johnstone says he would still be trying to measure what the State Department does, and for a simple reason: Foreign affairs is a $20 billion-a-year federal enterprise, and he thinks that the U.S. government ought to be able to offer some concrete evidence that the spending is worth it.

In wrestling the abstract world of diplomacy into forms that might be measured, Johnstone's approach is instructive, particularly for those who might legitimately be drawing a blank as to how to begin measuring any of what they do. The key, initially, argues Johnstone, is to insist that those who work in the organization articulate exactly what they think they are supposed to be accomplishing day in and day out. When it comes to inspiring people to come up with that kind of list, Johnstone takes a very pragmatic approach: "There's some reason why your program gets funded. So start listing those reasons. If you're too scared to do that, then maybe you shouldn't be getting the money."

Some of the areas in which Johnstone believes the State Department has an obligation to gauge U.S. impact include: ensuring that local and regional instabilities don't threaten the United States or its allies; boosting U.S. exports; reducing global population growth; and reducing global pollution. All of them are now listed as U.S. international relations goals, and progress toward all of them is now in the process of being measured (see "Performing Internationally" at the end of this chapter).

But not only does Johnstone think that goal-setting and performance measurement are appropriate and feasible in the international relations arena, he did the Government Performance and Results Act one better. As mentioned earlier, GPRA requires that every single department submit a strategic plan to Congress. To Johnstone, that didn't make a whole lot of sense in the international arena, inasmuch as a lot of different U.S. departments have direct impact on international relations (this intermingling of influence is true, of course, of many program areas in government—federal, state and local—and the more sophisticated performance measurement efforts will acknowledge and apportion to each some allotment of responsibility). And so Johnstone did something that GPRA didn't require (but, as he notes, probably should have): He insisted that all key federal agencies and departments that have significant impact on foreign affairs— whether the Peace Corps, the Agency for International Development or the Commerce Department—be formally tied into the State Department's overall strategic plan.

So if—as you begin to try to bring some tangibility to

what it is your shop does—you get stuck, consider what the State Department is up against. In an area where cause and effect can be murky, at best, where human behavior is core, and in which lots of unpredictable players have some influence (whether the player is Mother Nature, a group of partisan fanatics with automatic weapons and high explosives or a gaggle of wet-behind-the-ears Peace Corps volunteers), the department has begun to try to gauge where and to what extent it does have influence. By comparison, performance measurement in social services, higher ed and economic development would seem pretty simple to do.

Wonks and Final Frontiers

There are two other areas that tend to throw performance measurement gurus into a state of despair when it comes to trying to develop performance measures: preventive and research programs.

The assertion about preventive programs—pollution prevention, disease prevention, crime prevention, fire prevention and so forth—is sort of comically academic. You can't, the gurus will argue, measure what hasn't happened.

There's a perverse truth to this assertion, particularly when considered in a political context. Any given legislature looking for a place to make a budget cut might focus on some program or other that is clearly obsolete, inasmuch as the air is now all clean, polio and tuberculosis have been virtually eradicated, and nobody gets mugged around here anymore.

But ultimately, the argument that you can't measure what you've prevented is kind of silly and should probably be summarily dismissed. Obviously, if your locality is spending $60,000 a year on "meteor collision prevention," you might want to try cutting the budget in half just to see what happens. If what you're doing is trying to prevent pollution, disease or crime, on the other hand, you might want to consider cuts a little more carefully. Besides, the fact is that you frequently *can* measure the effect of preventive programs by looking at sustained reductions in rates of those things that you're trying to prevent. Those reductions, while perhaps not affirmative indicators of accomplishment, certainly tell policy makers something about the impact of what government is doing. In the wonkier reaches of the performance measurement world, these are called "surrogate" measures, but they'll sure sound like results to Jane and Joe Schmo.

As for research, that's another area where the world might be giving government too much of a bye. Lots of companies spend huge sums of money—technology and pharmaceutical companies, for example—on research every year. They expect something in return: new and improved products, and, at some point down the road, higher profits.

If the United States government is appropriating lots of money for research on AIDS, it's not unreasonable to expect that those institutions receiving the money at some point offer some evidence that they're making some progress (as, indeed, they have been). Certainly Uncle Sam can't require that X number of major medical or technological breakthroughs be delivered every fiscal year for X amount of dollars; failure is obviously an important part of research. But at the end of the day, or the end of the decade, there ought to be some reckoning for why the money was spent.

Chapter Five Quick Quiz

1. The argument that what you do is "unmeasurable" is probably going to:
   a. lead to some very interesting discussion come budget hearings time.
   b. inspire policy makers to have your program audited shortly after budget hearings time (see Chapter Seven).
   c. get you reassigned to a job where what you do *is* measurable.

2. The argument that what you do is "unmeasurable" is probably *not* going to:
   a. work.
   b. sell.
   c. fly.
   d. all the above

3. A logical first step in trying to develop good outcome measures for what it is you do might be to:
   a. figure out who your internal and/or external customers are and what it is they expect you to deliver/accomplish.
   b. talk to staff about what it is *they* think they're supposed to be accomplishing in the short and long run.
   c. find some operation similar to yours that has implemented a performance measurement program and swipe it.
   d. all of the above.

Performing Internationally

Below, the Strategic Plan for International Affairs as developed by the U.S. Department of State, including a representative sampling of performance indicators (this author's parentheticals added in some cases for explanation/clarification). Performance measurement experts will no doubt quibble with some of State's goals and outcome indicators. For example some might characterize the State Department goal "Expand exports, open markets, assist American businesses, foster economic growth and promote sustainable development" as internally contradictory. Others will wonder why State is concerning itself with the spread of disease. And as a performance indicator under the "Strategic Goal" of "Significantly reduce from 1997 levels the entry of illegal drugs into the United States," State includes "Disruption of drug group activities, as shown by arrests, prosecutions, convictions, asset seizures, and other law enforcement data," an arguably *output*-heavy performance measure. But State Department officials don't claim that their strategic plan is perfect, merely a work in progress.

MISSION STATEMENT:

The purpose of the United States Foreign Policy is to create a more secure, prosperous and democratic world for the benefit of the American people. In an increasingly interdependent and rapidly changing world, international events affect every American. Successful U.S. International leadership is essential to security at home, better jobs and a higher

standard of living, a healthier environment, and safe
travel and conduct of business abroad.

The goals of United States foreign policy are to:

1. Secure peace, deter aggression, prevent and defuse
   and manage crises, halt the proliferation of weapons
   of mass destruction, and advance arms control and
   disarmament.
2. Expand exports, open markets, assist American
   businesses, foster economic growth and promote sustainable development.
3. Protect American citizens abroad and safeguard the
   borders of the United States.
4. Combat international terrorism, crime, and nar-
   cotics trafficking.
5. Support the establishment and consolidation of
   democracies, and uphold human rights.
6. Provide humanitarian assistance to victims of crisis
   and disaster.
7. Improve the global environment, stabilize world population growth, and protect human health.

**"U.S. National Interests and Strategic Goals"
that flow from the seven overarching foreign
policy goals, including a sample indicator/
performance measure for each one
(with explanation, when necessary):**

1. Ensure that local and regional instabilities do not
   threaten the security and well-being of the United
   States or its allies.
   Sample indicator: Crises prevented, defused or
   solved.
2. Eliminate the threat to the United States and its

allies from weapons of mass destruction...and destabilizing conventional arms.

> **Sample indicator:** Progress in securing or disposing of excess fissile material.

3. Open foreign markets to free the flow of goods, services, and capital.

> **Sample indicator:** Conclusion of Open Skies agreements.

4. Expand U.S. Exports to $1.2 trillion by 2000.

> **Sample indicator:** Overall levels of U.S. exports of goods and services.

5. Increase global economic growth.

> **Sample indicator:** Incidence of financial crisis and economic instability.

6. Promote broad-based economic growth in developing and transitional economies.

> **Sample indicator:** Per capita GDP.

7. Enhance the ability of American citizens to live and travel abroad securely.

> **Sample indicator:** Availability and levels of use of consular information systems.

8. Control how immigrants and foreign visitors enter and remain in the United States.

> **Sample indicator:** Fees charged by alien smugglers (based on data that indicate fees increase as interdiction efforts get more effective).

9. Minimize the impact of international crime on the United States and its citizens.

> **Sample indicator:** Foreign government adherence to its own legislation, or other commitments to take action against transnational crime.

10. Significantly reduce from 1997 levels the entry of illegal drugs into the United States.

> **Sample indicator:** Disruption of drug group activities, as shown by arrests, prosecutions, con-

victions, asset seizures, and other law enforcement data.

11. Reduce international terrorist attacks, especially on the United States and its citizens.

   Sample indicator: Trends in international terrorism worldwide, including attacks against American targets, and the number of casualties.

12. Increase foreign government adherence to democratic practices and respect for human rights.

   Sample indicator: Evaluations of human rights practices and actions to prevent or mitigate human rights abuses.

13. Prevent or minimize the human costs of conflict and natural disasters.

   Sample indicator: Status of land mine cleanup and removal efforts.

14. Secure a sustainable global environment in order to protect the United States and its citizens from the effects of international environmental degradation.

   Sample indicator: Rate of increase in atmospheric greenhouse gas concentrations in the atmosphere.

15. Stabilize world population growth by 2020.

   Sample indicator: Female education levels (based on data that indicate better-educated women have fewer children).

16. Protect human health and reduce the spread of infectious diseases.

   Sample indicator: Disease outbreak response capabilities and performance.

CHAPTER SIX

Performance's Pesky Partner: Efficiency; Or How to Blow Things Up for Cheap

few years back, a certain reporter for a certain national magazine that covers state and local government wrote a glowing report about the performance of a certain big city's trash truck maintenance operation. OK, not exactly the kind of thing that was likely to win him a Pulitzer Prize or even make the shrine on his Mom's refrigerator door, but for those who are wise enough to see the true excitement of big-city trash hauling, it was quite an interesting piece.

In that item, this reporter outlined the incredible improvements that this maintenance department had made in the number of trucks it had road-ready every morning, as well as the incredible reductions in the time it took to get broken trucks back out on the street. This turnaround in performance by any measure was truly incredible, this reporter believed.

That was until a vigilant (overly vigilant in the reporter's opinion) consultant named Burt Jabri, who has made a career of consulting with big-city sanitation departments, dropped the reporter the kind of note that reporters really hate. In essence, the note said: With the kind of money this maintenance operation was spending, a monkey could have engineered the transformation. Dozens of other large municipalities, Jabri so painfully elaborated, did just as well at trash truck maintenance—and some even better—and for significantly less money.

The moral of that long-winded tale: Measuring performance is one thing; gauging whether that performance is cost-effective is quite another.

The reporter had just received his first lesson in the important concept of "efficiency" as fraternal twin to "effectiveness." A well-designed and well-implemented performance measurement effort won't just tell you whether or not you're effective—that is, whether you're getting the job that you're supposed to be doing done (and whether it's getting done better and better each year). It will *also* illuminate whether the resources (*inputs*) you're devoting to your incredibly effective efforts are reasonable, given the task at hand.

It's easy to be effective when you've got tons of money and staff to throw at a problem. The question is whether you're really getting your money's worth when you do that, or whether you might be able to make other adjustments to improve performance that don't necessarily involve simply upping your inputs, whether the input is money or people or new equipment.

The bottom line: *inputs* are as much a "performance measure" as *outcome indicators*. Both feed into the critical equation of how much bang you're getting for how many bucks.

Costing Out Potholes, Pipe and Those Double Yellow Lines You See When You Drive in Iowa

But getting at efficiency is tricky. It requires that governments analyze all the major costs associated with accomplishing certain tasks, and that can be complicated. Moving somebody from welfare to self-sufficiency, putting away a felon for life or quelling conflict in a regional hotspot can all be difficult activities to cost out.

Despite the potential complexities, though, an alchemy of cost accounting that allows government to do all that has begun to develop. That alchemy is known as "activity-based costing," or "ABC" to its practitioners. While ABC rolls off the tongue easily, implementing it can be anything but; it is only just emerging as an accounting technique with which anybody in government has much experience or expertise.

Most simply put, ABC is the practice of focusing on some unit of output—whether it's filling a pothole or sending a battle fleet to the Mediterranean or fixing a garbage truck's busted transmission—and then trying to figure out what that unit of output cost and what contributed to that cost, such as man (or "person," if you prefer) hours (including pension and medical benefits), materials and equipment, administrative overhead and beyond. With such a breakdown in hand, the theory of ABC goes, managers can home in on key cost drivers of the output that might be ripe for reduction.

Local governments have probably been at ABC the longest and with the most success. Indianapolis became famous (not famous like Tom Cruise, but famous among those who are keenly interested in such fascinating subjects as big-city trash hauling, road repair and sewer and water delivery) in 1992, when newly elected Mayor Steve Goldsmith asked what is probably the most fundamental question any local politician could ask: What does it cost the city to do specific things like fill one pothole or seal the cracks in a mile of road?

Nobody had the foggiest notion.

They do now. Sealing cracks in one lane-mile of an Indianapolis street costs $737.59. Labor accounts for $352.77 of that; materials, $62.05 ($58 of which is crumb rubber); equipment gobbles up $82.48; vehicles, $54.11; and overhead (including buildings and general administration), $186.18. The city has done the same thing for filling potholes ($39.87 per pothole, on average) and for doing a bunch of other stuff, as well. With such a breakdown in hand, Indianapolis has been able to do two things: pinpoint costs to cut and calculate whether contracting out any of the road repair makes sense.

Indeed, because of the detailed cost breakdown required by ABC, the better-run governments see it as the logical first step when trying to figure out whether to privatize a certain activity or function (other, not so well-run governments like to take it on faith that privatization will save them money, and apparently don't mind learning the hard way that it often doesn't). After all, how can you really do a request for proposals if you don't have a good idea what the per-unit cost of a service or product is, along with what contributes to that cost? (One thing that government is starting to learn, for example, is that a lot of administrative overhead costs are fixed, so that dumping some function or other onto the private sector may not actually lead to the expected huge savings.)

Fort Lauderdale used ABC back in 1996, when it was considering contracting out its municipal sewer and water pipe-laying operations. Using a very detailed formula, the city's public works department came up with a per-foot breakdown of pipe-laying expenses, apportioning that cost among salaries and benefits, materials, equipment, general administrative overhead and so forth. According to the analysis, it was costing the city $73 a foot to lay pipe.

With those figures in hand, the city did its RFP, getting a handful of responses back from private contractors. What the city discovered surprised public works managers more than a little bit: The private sector was ready and willing—

ready and willing, that is, to stick it to the city. Private contractor bids ranged from $100 to $130 per foot. And so Fort Lauderdale did several things. First, it chose not to contract the job out. Second, it used its cost breakdown to analyze areas in which the city could actually save more money in the pipe-laying process. For example, DPW front-line employees convinced the DPW brass that a lot of time was being wasted in hauling equipment and materials between the DPW garage and the job site. Now crews set up on site and leave equipment and materials there overnight so that workers can go straight to the job each morning. Third, the city decided to continue to monitor its per-foot costs. If the cost does start to creep up, the city will be ready to either investigate other possible efficiencies or perhaps reopen the discussion of contracting out.

So far, the cost of putting down pipe isn't going up, though; it's going down. According to the city's 1998 calculations, the city's per-foot pipe-laying cost is now below $50. It is worth noting that the private contractors' latest low bid is down too, to $69. It seems that government efficiency can infect even that sometimes bloated and backwards "good-enough-for-government-work" crowd known as the private sector.

Now there are two ways to go at ABC. There's "ballpark" ABC, which will give you a half-decent idea of what specific outputs are costing you just for your own information. And then there is highly detailed, all-encompassing ABC, which jurisdictions should use—as did Fort Lauderdale—if the data are actually going to be used to make a go/no-go decision on contracting out.

The difference between the two—and how to calculate them—is outlined in a nice concise paper co-authored by Mark Abrahams, a Massachusetts-based performance measurement consultant, and Mary Noss Reavely, project manager of Iowa's Council on Human Investment (the work of which was mentioned in the previous chapter). In "Activity Based Costing: Illustrations from the State of Iowa," Abrahams and Reavely cover how the Iowa DOT is now costing out line painting, and in impressive detail (for those who just have to know, center lines in Iowa cost $131.89 a mile, and edge lines cost $134.37 a mile, according to Abrahams and Reavely). But the paper also covers what the authors describe as the "keep-it-simple" method of cost accounting for those who don't need to know in excruciating detail what every unit of output costs them but who just want to get some idea on key costs driving some process or other. (For those who want to learn more about ABC and to get a copy of the Iowa DOT costing case study, see "If You're Still Serious..." at the end of this book.)

ABC and the Government Food Chain

Now, those of you who are astute and organized enough to still have on your desk that long list of things that government does that this book asked you to write during your lunch hour at the beginning of the previous chapter will correctly surmise that ABC tends to be a more straightforward proposition at the local-government level (or with state functions similar to what localities do, such as painting lines on highways). City, county, borough and wide-place-in-the-road governments tend to deliver hard, measurable services, such as trash collection or road repair or permits for running a business, all of which lend themselves to an ABC analysis. ABC gets to be a trickier proposition as you go up the governmental food chain, because as you go up, what government does, as a rule, gets more abstract.

But that hasn't stopped higher levels of government from trying. As outlined in an excellent and exciting article in the May 1997 issue of *Government Executive* magazine (but one that, alas, still didn't make the shrine on Mom's refrigerator door), ABC is actually beginning to catch on at the federal level, with a handful of agencies developing some fairly sophisticated ABC models.

Death Benefits by the Numbers

The Veterans Benefits Administration of the Department of Veterans Affairs has begun calculating the cost of activities related to key outputs, including processing life insurance benefits for survivors of veterans. The set of calculations that follows is for benefits administered by VA's Philadelphia Regional Office and Insurance Center. In fiscal year 1996, the office processed 134,285 death awards at a total administrative cost of $7,416,640, or $55.23 per transaction (the actual value of all those death awards is in the billions of dollars). According to Richard Norwood, project manager for activity based costing, the detailed breakdown of cost per transaction, presented below, will allow managers to much more accurately monitor and analyze any major fluctuations in the cost per unit of delivering death benefits from year to year, with an eye toward figuring out ways to make the operation as efficient as possible on a continuing basis.

The Cost of Dying (FY 1996)

The output: process 134,285 death benefit claims

ACTIVITY	COST
Receive and process incoming mail	$486,793
Research case files	426,693
Additional research for more-complex cases	78,993
Process and mail death award checks	4,031,204
Verify that checks were sent out	427,642
Spot-check the award and verification process	245,906
Customized (non-automated) claims disbursements	143,228
General follow-up on files and paperwork	234,479
Update or retire files	274,766
Information technology systems cost	1,066,936
	TOTAL COST: $7,416,640
TOTAL OUTPUTS PROCESSED: 134,285	**COST PER OUTPUT: $55.23**

The General Services Administration has been one of the most aggressive federal entities in pursuing ABC, and there are a couple of reasons why. The first, and most obvious, is that GSA provides direct and fairly concrete services, such as delivering office equipment and real-estate brokering. But the big reason GSA is pursuing ABC isn't that it's relatively easy for officials there to do it (in fact, it's been a lot of work). The biggest reason is that GSA has had to pursue ABC as a matter of long-term survival.

The fact is, GSA has been getting the stuffing kicked out of its budget and staffing levels over the past few years; both have been cut by 30 percent since 1993. In the face of that kind of pressure, top managers had a pretty logical epiphany: They decided that they had better start coming up with some new and creative ways to do what they do more efficiently, on the one hand, and start proving to Congress that they provide real value to government (and taxpayers) for the resources that they do get, on the other.

The problem came when GSA officials sat down to try to figure all that out. What they found was that when it came to calculating—or arguing—their own efficiency, they really didn't have the slightest idea what it actually cost to provide any of GSA's services on a transaction-by-transaction basis. Yes, they could come up with general numbers about GSA's annual budget and expenditures. They could produce reams of data on what the agency accomplished in any given year—leases signed, buildings bought and sold, and so forth. What they couldn't illustrate in any meaningful detail was what it cost to do those very specific things. GSA officials didn't know, in other words, whether the agency actually was—or could be—competitive with the private-sector real-estate office down the block. Or, and probably more to the point, whether GSA was providing real value to its immediate customer, the rest of the federal government.

But even if GSA guessed—or roughly calculated—that it could be more efficient and competitive, it still had a problem: It had no idea of the specific areas of expense that actually contributed to the overall cost of doing something like finding and renting office space for another government agency. How much of the cost was for personnel? How much was administrative overhead? How much could be apportioned to travel? How much was just redundant paper-pushing? Without such specific information, any effort to become more efficient would be flying blind.

It was GSA's Property Acquisition and Realty Service business line—essentially the real-estate arm of GSA—that stepped forward fastest when GSA's top brass first asked for internal ABC volunteers. While PARS is just starting to come up with full cost accountings of its various products and services, it has already used the ABC process to identify ways to do its job cheaper, faster and smarter. For example, it has already streamlined its lease and purchase process by eliminating redundant steps.

Like its parent agency, PARS had a good reason for stepping forward to be among the first to try ABC: It is the division within GSA that is most under the privatization gun. Whether or not PARS is competitive with Joe & Moe's Realty across town is still an open question, but at least PARS is beginning to get a fix on the answer.

As always, there will be those who will argue that much of what government does—the federal government in particular—defies even ballpark attempts at activity-based costing. And those who believe that will once again have to contend with Ambassador Craig Johnstone at the State Department.

He acknowledges that applying ABC to international affairs ain't easy. For example, he points out that translators often wind up serving beyond their capacities as mere unscramblers of information; they frequently end up developing key expertise in certain program areas, and they often develop important relationships with foreign dignitaries that have value beyond the narrow job description of translator. Therefore, apportioning the cost of training translators to a particular program area or goal might not really capture a translator's ultimate value to the overall international relations enterprise. "What we've elected to do is attribute things like salary or training costs to our 16 strategic goals when it's reasonable to do that," says Johnstone. "But if it's not reasonable, then we put it into a more general category, like 'diplomatic readiness.'"

So we're back to that loathsome refrain: If you work for the U.S. EPA or a state department of social services and you feel like arguing that it's impossible to apportion costs to promoting clean air or moving people from welfare to work, think about what Ambassador Johnstone is tackling.

Oh, blowing things up: The Navy's new battle cruisers actually have on-board computers that calculate the cheapest alternative when locking on to one military target or another. Once the target has been identified, the computer sorts through its choices of projectile and chooses the most miserly missile for the job. This is sort of a preemptive form of ABC, one that should be comforting to U.S. taxpayers, if not to certain Middle East despots.

Chapter Six Quick Quiz

1. Some of NASA's costs associated with naming rocks on Pluto after famous cartoon characters might include:
   a. fuel required to get your spacecraft within rock-naming range.
   b. paper and pens for writing down which rocks were named what.
   c. the cost of retraining astronauts to be proficient rock-namers.

2. To figure out the efficiency of your rock-naming program, some possible calculations might include:
   a. cost of fuel divided by number of rocks successfully named.

b. per-rock pension costs for the team that thought up rock-naming as one of NASA's important goals.

c. NASA's total budget divided by the number of U.S. citizens who answer "Yes" to the statement: "My place in the solar system feels less mysterious and more secure now that I know there's a rock on Pluto named 'Goofy.' "

3. You might want to contract out your rock-naming effort when:

a. Acme Intergalactic Rock Naming, Inc., undercuts your per-unit cost of rock naming by at least 25 percent.

b. you've decided that intergalactic rock naming should no longer be NASA's chief mission.

c. you want to make the jump to the private sector.

CHAPTER SEVEN

Key Principles of Public Management: Lying, Cheating and Bumbling

nyone who has spent any time in and around government realizes that, ultimately, a lot of the cumbersome rules and regulations that have grown up around public administration are based on a powerful and fundamental truth about human nature: Some people take certain liberties with the truth; others take certain liberties with public assets; still others like to take shortcuts in their work in a way that's not conducive to the collective good; others are well-meaning but bumbling; and some are simply clueless. It's a small percentage of people in all, but they manage to cause inconvenience and damage wildly disproportionate to their actual numbers.

And they are why auditors were invented.

Given the data-intensive nature of measuring performance, and given the drive to make the data mean something as far as program and budget decisions go, there is obviously going to be some temptation to be creative when it comes to reporting results. "There are lots of honest mistakes," says Martha Marshall, one of Prince William County, Virginia's, performance gurus, "and then there are those mistakes where you wonder. Clearly, as more and more emphasis is put on performance measures in making program and budget decisions, you could anticipate a situation where a program director or manager might feel inclined to pump up the numbers."

Marshall hastens to add that the inclination to fudge or not fudge numbers will, as a rule, occur in direct proportion to how the numbers are used by upper-level managers and policy makers: If performance measures are honestly used to help people be more efficient and effective, then honesty will likely be the standard policy when it comes to reporting results. However, if performance measures are used mostly to judge and punish, expect a little creativity around reporting time. In early 1998, the chief of the New York City transit police was accused by police department upper brass of sliding certain subway crimes onto aboveground precincts in order to boost his own on-paper performance. Speculation, at the time, was that the transit chief did this to avoid the type of browbeating that top cops get from the upper brass in the New York City PD when performance numbers slip.

It's a point worth emphasizing. The whole idea behind performance measurement is to improve government service and increase public trust in government performance. The way to do that, obviously, is to use performance indicators constructively. As we'll see in the next chapter, there are going to be times when a program's performance may be judged to be so bad that the only thing to do is pull its plug—or at least cut way back on the juice. But in the vast majority of cases, performance measures are—theoretically—going to be used to support that management holy grail known as "continuous improvement."

Helping Elected Officials to Get It

But those working in government need to be convinced that performance measurement is really going to be used to help them before there's going to be any widespread acceptance of the practice. People have to be reassured that by joining in the pursuit of performance measurement, they are not building the very vehicle that ultimately is going to be used to run them over. Chances are that mid- and upper-level career managers in government understand the dynamic: Management reform has to be applied in a way that's used to support people and not undercut them. High-level appointees sweeping into some new management position might need to be reminded that this is the goal of performance measurement. But the group that really needs to get the message is elected officials, particularly those of the grandstanding persuasion, for they are the ones who will be most inclined to publicly berate poor performers as a way to boost their own standing in the political pecking order.

Now, before public officials—elected or otherwise—can be expected to do the right thing with performance measurement data, it is not unreasonable for them to ask for some assurance that the information they're getting is valid and verifiable. Which is where auditors come in...or should come in.

There is a debate within the auditing community right now over exactly what a government auditor's role should be in reviewing performance measurement programs. Auditors, generally, aren't crazy about being called in to double-check the accuracy of performance data, and there is a simple reason for that reluctance. In many cases, performance data isn't like budget data—hard numbers on a printout. For some performance indicators, results may be a bit ambiguous. When is a welfare case closed? When is a criminal case closed? When is a developmentally disabled adult "job-ready"? When is an estuary "clean"? How do you define "regional peace"? How do you assess the validity of data on worldwide fertility rates?

That is why bringing auditors into the whole performance measurement process after the fact—the typical governmental approach—has tended to cause two problems: First, discomfort on the part of the auditors, generally, with the whole and new notion of auditing performance measures, because they've never been asked to do such a thing before. Second, a lack of clarity in the auditor's mind about what constitutes "performance" and "results" in any given instance.

So it is probably worth pulling auditors into the whole performance measurement process right from the get-go. On the one hand, it gets them comfortable with the whole concept of auditing something other than financial data; on the other, notes Jim Webster, chief internal auditor for Prince William County, it allows auditors and program managers to work out cooperatively what exactly is being measured (and therefore what exactly is being verified come audit time).

Your Results Aren't My Results

In pursuing regular audits of his county departments, Webster discovered early on that departments with high rates of unverifiable data weren't intentionally screwing up the numbers, it's just that the auditor and the program manager didn't agree on what information certain indicators were really trying to capture. Was response time, for example, the interlude between the 911 call and the arrival on the scene? Or was it the time between the squad car's being dispatched by the 911 center and its arrival on the scene? Was a case closed when a suspect was arrested, or was it closed when somebody was convicted? "I think if we had to do it all over again, my office would have been much more closely involved in defining the indicators," says Webster.

But that's a notion that really makes the traditionalists in the auditing community squirm. If some of them are uncomfortable even reviewing such non-financial and sometimes ambiguous data as that contained in some performance measures, even more of them are positively spooked by the idea of actually *venturing an opinion* as to whether the outcome indicator itself is a good measure of what the operation in question is actually trying to accomplish.

Clearly, the best and brightest in the auditing community think auditors do need to expand their role beyond such exciting activities as chasing expense vouchers through filing cabinets. "Accuracy of performance data is all well and good, but if the measure isn't valid in the first place, what's the point?" says one of the U.S. General Accounting Office's top auditors, who asked for anonymity lest she find herself on the front page of the *Washington Post* for speaking out so boldly on such a high-profile topic of daily national controversy.

But even if auditors begin to accept this new role, there is, naturally, one other big worry: that they will start stepping on the toes of those who do program and policy evaluation (something like having your local H&R Block tax preparer report to you on April 15th not the bottom-line results of your Form 1040, but rather that you have lousy work habits and need to dress better for success).

The debate over the proper role of the auditor aside, the auditing community in general is clearly starting to lean more toward increased involvement in the whole performance measurement game. Already the government audit community is churning out "exposure drafts" that float the proposition that auditors might actually have a legitimate role in evaluating indicators ("exposure drafts," for those of you unfamiliar with the wonderful world of auditing, are the auditing community's way of sneaking up—very slowly and painfully deliberatively—on the obvious and the inevitable).

Ultimately, auditors don't have any choice, thinks Nora Masters, who used to be chief auditor for the city of Seattle but who was recently hired away by one of the big private accounting firms. "If we're asked to come in and only look at the quality of the numbers, but we see a big problem with the quality of the indicator, then I think we have a professional responsibility to say something about it."

Masters has high-level backing in service efforts and accomplishments reporting (remember that SEA reporting is the two-dollar term for "activities and results") from Dick Tracy—not the impossibly square-jawed comic-strip detective (though what a fine performance auditor he would make) but the auditor of Portland, Oregon, who's recognized as a real SEA guru. "I think an audit is incomplete without looking at whether the measures are relevant," says Tracy. By relevant, Tracy means that they actually measure results. Again, some operations can be producing reams of data, and that data might be very accurate, but it also might have nothing to do with outcomes. For example, the U.S. Department of Education might be able to report with great accuracy how much money it has dispensed in grants in a year and to whom. But if an auditor is asked to verify such a number as an *outcome indicator*, he or she should flag the fact that such spending is an *output* and not an *outcome*. Now, there is nothing wrong with measuring outputs; in fact, it is critical that outputs be measured. (Indeed, they, like *inputs*, are a type of performance measure, and data on them should be judiciously and religiously collected as part of any performance measurement effort.) They just shouldn't be confused with results. So any conscientious auditor who is asked to verify a number on grant moneys dispensed, or fines collected, or kids graduated, or troops sent to the Middle East, or vaccination shots given in a year as *outcome indicators* should point out that all those are meant, hopefully, to influence outcome indicators, but they aren't outcome indicators themselves.

Tracy is careful, though, to draw the line between judging indicators and judging a program's overall mission or whether it is pursuing that mission in a sensible fashion. "There is a point beyond which we shouldn't go," says Tracy. "I don't think auditors should be involved in a discussion of goals or mission or vision. But I do think that we should look to see whether the indicators an agency chooses flow logically from those goals or mission."

Auditors and Their Future Employability

Whatever individual auditors may think about this—a lot of them still don't like the idea of messing about in this new area—the issue has probably already been decided, at least from the standpoint of future employability. While there may be some foot-dragging and whining, auditors who don't get with the performance picture probably don't have a very promising future in the profession.

The more fundamental fact is that a small cadre of auditors at the state and local government level has for years been doing evaluations of performance that go well beyond a hard look at financial data. And a very large cadre of auditors at the federal level—better known as the U.S. General Accounting Office—long ago decided it was stupid to ask auditors to certify financial statements but ignore the broader performance of the entity being audited.

And so for quite a while now, state, local and federal agencies, departments and programs have been the subject of what are known in auditing jargon as "performance audits." Rather than just check on dollars in/dollars out, performance auditors delve into organizational design and function on a wide front to evaluate whether an operation is efficient and effective. From how well staffed, equipped, managed and successful fire departments are to whether welfare-to-work programs are actually moving people off the dole and into jobs in an efficient way, state, local and federal auditors are assuming a much more involved and activist role in calculating whether taxpayers are really getting their money's worth.

Now, a *performance audit* should not be confused with the *auditing of performance indicators*. The former is a comprehensive look at the efficiency and effectiveness of some function of government; the latter is purely a look at the accuracy of the data and the quality and of the indicators that some entity or other is using to gauge its own performance.

Nightmare on Elmwood Street

For a good street-level example of a *performance audit*, Kansas City, Missouri's city auditor, Mark Funkhouser, has a favorite tale that he calls "Nightmare on Elmwood Street." It is derived from a performance audit his office did of the coordination between the city's public works department and the local utility companies around the issue of utility cuts—the holes that gas, water and electric companies punch through the pavement in order to put in and work on underground pipes and cables.

In the three years covered by his study, Funkhouser's office calculated that the cuts cost Kansas City $4.4 million, an amount that wasn't even remotely covered by the permit fees the city was charging utilities. Worse, utilities seemed to ignore entirely city repaving schedules in making their own decisions about where and when to dig.

Enter Elmwood Street. After being assured by the local gas utility that it had no plans to dig up Elmwood anytime soon, the city went ahead with a $22,000 resurfacing project. Within months of the project's completion, the gas company showed up and jackhammered 44 holes in the new tar. The damage total came to $7,300—or $7,281 more than the amount covered by the utility's $19 permit fee.

Funkhouser issued a tough report on the idiocy of the situation, a report that quickly got the city council's attention. The council voted to boost permit fees and also to create a system for recovering any higher costs of damage from utility cuts.

In the case above, it was the utilities that wound up hating Funkhouser, but usually it's the governmental agency or department that's the subject of the audit that gets ticked off. In fact, a lot of agency and department managers don't care for performance audits at all. They don't want some glorified bean counter with big ideas about efficient government coming in and poking and prying into every corner of their operation.

But absent the regular production of clear, certifiable and timely performance data, any agency or department that is spending significant amounts of taxpayer dollars in an area of any significant importance to the overall work of their government is just asking for a performance audit, whether they want one or not.

And so the smart manager will quickly realize there is one good way to inoculate her or his department from being subjected to such prying: Bring an auditor in in the first place to help the department develop clear, timely and certifiable performance measurement data (including data related to outcomes, outputs and inputs). And then invite your friendly neighborhood auditors in regularly to verify that data, because they're going to be paying you a visit sooner or later, one way or the other. The visit might as well be on your terms.

It is also a good way to signal to your local auditor that you, personally, are not a liar, cheater or bumbler (nor clueless), and that you're interested in curbing—even forestalling—the aforementioned damage that can be done by those who are.

Chapter 7 Quick Quiz

1. When you see an auditor wandering down the hall in your direction, it's time to:
   a. research international extradition treaties and buy a ticket to a country with which the U.S. doesn't have one.
   b. sneak out of the office by pretending you're just any other front-line staffer on his way to lunch.
   c. invite them in for a look around and keep your fingers crossed that they really are there to help.

2. You know that an auditor is there to help when:
   a. they're being trailed by two police officers
   b. they wear their pocket calculators in holsters.
   c. they call ahead.

3. You know that the elected politicians in your jurisdiction understand the value of certified clean performance data when:
   a. they leak numbers indicating sub-par performance to the press and then use the publicity to run for higher office.
   b. in the wake of some bad numbers, they hire a big-money, big-name auditing firm to come in and straighten you out.
   c. in the wake of some bad numbers, they ask you what you need to do the job better.

4. You know that upper-level management understands the value of certified clean performance data when:
   a. they ask you to shred all copies of the latest performance report.
   b. in the wake of some bad numbers, they hire a big-

money, big-name auditing firm to come in and cook the books for you.

c. in the wake of some bad numbers, they ask you what you need to do the job better.

5. You know your local press understands the purpose of certified clean performance data when:
   a. they jacklight you on the back steps of your office building and ask you how long you've been stealing pens and paper clips from the supply room.
   b. they run a story comparing your performance to the performance of that mythical local government known in public administration lore as "Sunnyvale," California.
   c. the reporter they send to interview you about the latest performance measurement data is not young enough to be your great grandson/daughter and actually seems to understand such complex concepts of government as the difference between the legislative and the executive branch.

CHAPTER EIGHT

Performance-Based Budgeting in the Real World

Performance measurement is the proud father of twins: They are "performance management" and "performance-based budgeting." Any discussion of performance measurement needs to deal with these two intertwined branches of the performance measurement family.

Let's dispense with "performance management" first. Which is to say, we're not going to spend much time on it at all; if you really believe that you can't live without a lengthy and detailed explanation of performance management, you can hire a $1,000-a-day consultant (the author is available, and will be far more entertaining than the drone in the suit) to unravel for you the mysteries of the practice.

But, briefly, we'll spill the beans about what you'll get when you shell out that thousand bucks, and at the bargain-basement price of what it cost you to buy this book: The $1,000-a-day consultant you hire to cover the magical world of performance management will deliver the following jaw-dropping news to you and your staff: In order to be a "high-performance organization," you must: (a) have some idea of what it is you're supposed to be accomplishing in both the short and long run (and in the context of changing future circumstances and demands); (b) have a short-term and long-term plan for how to accomplish that; and (c) develop some way to gauge and report progress (or lack thereof) toward those accomplishments. The consultant will also tell you that you need "buy in" from upper-level management, that you need to "empower" your employees, "flatten" your organization, listen to your "customers," quit focusing on "outputs" and start focusing on "results." If you're really lucky, the consultant will fire up his PowerPoint software and slap a flow chart up on the wall that's reminiscent of a Jackson Pollock painting. As a bonus, some consultants might even tell you that you need to "think outside the box" or "color outside the lines"—just the sort of sophisticated management advice you expect to get for $1,000 a day.

In explaining all of this, the consultant will also probably use a lot of those words we covered in Chapter Three, including "mission," "outcomes," "benchmarks" and "goals," and he or she will throw in a few others, such as "strategic planning" and "visioning." And of course the consultant will also use that word that we so studiously avoided in our lexicological discussion in Chapter Three (and everywhere else in this book, for that matter): "paradigm," which you will be called upon to shift (apparently, paradigms, even in this advanced technological age, still don't come in an automatic). These are, to digress even further, all the words that $1,000-a-day consultants have been using since 1234 B.C. (when, incidentally, they also charged $1,000 a day in inflation-adjusted silver talents).

Now, none of the above is meant to imply that performance management isn't a good thing to do. It is a wonderful thing to do. It's just that carving it out as some sort of new, exotic management strategy is a little silly; one of the goals implicit in any performance measurement effort is to encourage reevaluation of management systems in light of results—results desired and results achieved. In fact, most governments that have pursued performance measurement in any kind of sensible way have quickly discovered that the practice has immediate and positive impacts on how programs run and policies are carried out. Once focused on accomplishments, new (or redirected) pathways to those accomplishments start becoming clear. Indeed, some performance measurement experts, such as Jay Fountain at the Governmental Accounting Standards Board, argue that in pursuing any performance measurement effort you are, in fact, doing performance management—it's the measures that underpin it.

So we highly endorse the idea of management systems driven by results. But we also argue that such a system is implicit in any performance measurement effort. If it isn't, why bother with any of this stuff in the first place?

Smoking Budgets

Performance-based budgeting is another bag of smoke altogether, and we'll start with a short anecdote by way of illustration:

In the fall of 1993, Mississippi sent a contingent of state lawmakers to Austin, Texas, to attend a major conference on performance measurement in the public sector. What the group hoped to learn all about was an approach to budgeting that was 180 degrees different from the old-style, line-item, input-based budgets that they were used to doing, budgets that were calculated through some combination of factors including last year's budget, the pleadings of department directors and their supporting special interests, the crisis du jour and the political skill and power of legislative angels.

Using the radically new budgeting strategy being discussed in Austin, resources allocated to a government department would depend on something entirely new: in some part on what the department had accomplished the previous year and in large part what it hoped to accomplish in the upcoming year (or two, if you operate on a biennial budget). It was brilliant in its logic and simplicity: If governments would start basing spending on what they want to accomplish rather than on such factors as those listed in the previous paragraph, then "results" would begin to drive the budget process, not politics.

For Mississippi state Representative George Flaggs Jr., who attended the Austin conference, the implications were obvious and powerful. No longer would Mississippi continue to spend the same old money on the same old ineffective programs, programs that for years had failed to pull the state out of its perennial position as national cellar-dweller in such categories of societal well-being as school dropout rates, crime and economic development. Presented with data on results, the state's political power brokers would be forced to face the fact that they were currently spending money to very poor effect and that they needed to either change the programs or change the funding levels going to those programs, or both. "This circumvents the political power," Flaggs asserted. "This allows change because you're dealing with objective measures rather than subjective ones."

Back home, Representative Flaggs and his colleagues pushed a performance-based budgeting bill through the legislature, a bill that promised to transform the whole budget, program and policy-shaping process in Jackson. It would tie dollars to outcomes and thereby begin to squeeze politics out of the budgeting process.

The problem is that five years later, the state still isn't doing anything remotely like comprehensive performance-based budgeting.

But it's not fair to single out Mississippi as one of the governments struggling with performance-based budgeting, and for two reasons: First, because they're still working on their performance-based budgeting phase-in, and so it's too early to declare defeat or victory; and second, hardly any other government in the U.S. has had much luck implementing performance-based budgeting, either. (In fact, governmental lore would have it that the only place that such a comprehensive performance-based budgeting program may actually exist is in that mythical local government with the obviously made-up name of "Sunnyvale," California, where elected officials and executive staff are said to figure up a budget based not on line items and the latest revenue reports but rather on reams of data on outcomes, outputs and inputs, all crunched to evaluate program performance in relation to long-term governmental and community goals—something like how Brigadoon would be run if Brigadoon had a city manager.)

Swelling Indicators

Mythology notwithstanding, there are a handful of real places that are making real progress toward something like performance-based budgeting. But these places are mostly local governments (where the connection between resources and results tends to be easier to make), and implementation is far from comprehensive, at least at this point.

Prince William County, Virginia, is as far along as any government in doing real performance-based budgeting, and here is how it can work in reality: In 1997, the county cut the budget of a local drug rehabilitation program because the program wasn't performing up to expectations. According to Craig S. Gerhart, deputy county executive, performance data indicated that only 25 percent of the program's clients were actually completing the whole course of treatments. While astute readers who've made it this far in this book realize immediately that participation rates aren't technically "outcomes" by the strict definition of performance measures, but "outputs," county budgeters were comfortable making the logical leap: If 75 percent of clients are dropping out of the program before they even finish, the program outcome of getting people off drugs is probably not being well served. And so the decision wasn't very hard to make, says Gerhart. "We said, 'We're not interested in buying that level of service. Let's put our money in another program.'" And when it came time to pass a new budget, the county council agreed.

While certain localities like Prince William County are clearly making progress in the whole area of performance-based budgeting, no state government is really there yet, although several are making interesting progress. Meanwhile, the federal government is closer to Pluto than it is to doing anything like performance-based budgeting. (In fact, anybody who actually believes that the Government Performance and Results Act is going to drive budget decisions on Capitol Hill probably also thinks that *Mr. Smith Goes to Washington* was a true story; in fact, they probably think that Jimmy Stewart really was once a member of Congress.)

Certainly some legislators—even federal-level ones— are aware that such a thing as performance-based budgeting is reported to exist. And in a number of states and localities, budget documents are indeed starting to swell with indicators that present performance levels and performance goals in some relation to the resources that have been allocated in the past and that are being requested for the future.

And several states are trying hard to move their budgets more toward a results base. But it isn't easy. "The generic problem is that the culture of government is more comfortable focusing on process," says Marv Weidner, Iowa Governor Terry Branstad's point man on performance. "Most laws governing policy and governing appropriations don't speak to end results, they speak to process, like how many people work for government and how many people they serve."

Six years into its push for performance-based budgeting, Iowa's goal for the effort is still modest and admirably realistic: "We would like budget discussions to shift to the results we are after and how to measure those results instead of 'How many copy machines do we need on the fifth floor,' " says Weidner. "So our first result is to change the discussion." It's slow going, Weidner concedes. But at least in Iowa the discussion is moving forward. A more cautionary tale comes courtesy of Florida, which embarked on its performance-based budgeting effort around the same time.

Messy, Messy Politics

On paper, Florida's performance-based budgeting effort was looking pretty good. For example, when Florida's Division of Community Colleges submitted its annual "performance-based legislative program budget request" for Fiscal Year 1998, it was packed with numbers on how many community college students went on to four-year schools, the percentage of graduates who passed licensing exams, time to degree, retention and graduation rates, data on student debt, and data on hours that faculty spend teaching, among a host of other performance measures.

But whether or not Florida legislators paid any attention to such data when making their budget decisions is another question altogether. The evidence is that they did not.

"It's just a lot easier to use measures for internal management purposes than 'We're going to give you money for outcomes,' " says Karen Stanford, who *used* to be executive director of the Florida Commission on Governmental Accountability to the People (called the "GAP Commission"), the citizen board that *used* to oversee the state's performance-based budgeting effort. In a world where budgets actually were tied to outcomes, says Stanford, "that would mean giving up some control, and legislators don't want to do that."

In fact, in Florida, there was apparently so little interest in doing that that the legislature recently de-funded the

GAP Commission (which it had created), arguing that other entities in government were producing the same sorts of numbers, so the commission's work was duplicative and the spending on it was unnecessary. Given that the $200,000 that the state saved by pulling the commission's plug doesn't even amount to a rounding error in the state's $48 billion budget, one does have to wonder if there wasn't some other reason for the legislature's eagerness to disappear the GAP Commission.

Well, it turns out there was, and it is a cautionary tale: Not only did legislators not want to give up budget control, they didn't want to give up their seats in the legislature, either. As the GAP Commission began to gather and analyze performance data—and also critique the quality of the state's overall performance measurement and performance budgeting systems—it was, among other things, sometimes releasing information critical of the pet projects of various legislators. And such information was occasionally being used by election challengers. "It was dynamite stuff," says one Florida political operative, who used commission data to help run an opposition legislative campaign.

It is unlikely that incumbent legislators anywhere are going to willingly continue funding what amounts to opposition intelligence for very long. And conceivably, the Florida incident helps explain, in part, why legislators generally have seemed less than enthusiastic about the idea of developing detailed (or easily accessible) information on performance: Just as the legislature can use the information to browbeat public administrators, the material can be used to beat up on legislators and their favorite programs.

In Florida, performance-based budgeting isn't dead, but it's not exactly dancing, either.

The most fundamental stumbling block to performance-based budgeting, however, probably isn't that data can be used to hurt incumbents, generally, or to criticize the highway-to-nowhere project that one or the other has managed to win for his or her district, specifically (even if all of that to win for his or her district, specifically (even if all of that might be in the back of legislators' minds as they consider the prospect of performance measurement). The most fundamental stumbling block continues to be the question of whether legislatures in general—at the federal, local or state level—are going to begin making "rational" budget decisions based on performance data when the culture of legislative budgeting is so steeped in business as usual.

Anybody who has watched any legislative body in action for any amount of time knows that "results" are only one ingredient—and a very mutable one, at that—in the larger budget decision stew, the other ingredients being pork, power politics, polling data, dubious (or at best unsubstantiated) ideas about what works and what doesn't, influence trading, and what horror story happens to be flashing across the tube during the 6 o'clock news at the moment, just to name a few in the ever-shifting and complex recipe.

Indeed, when it comes to the realities of textbook performance-based budgeting, Lisa Schumaker, budget analyst with the city of Charlotte, North Carolina, wins the prize for frankness. "It is not uncommon for staff to lay out the story to the city council on the achievements of some program," says Schumacher, "and it's not a very pretty story. And the policy makers will thank us for our input and tell us that for these reasons, they have to continue funding it. Our conscience is clear, we shared the performance information with them. It's their prerogative what to do with it."

How It Can Work for You

Now, none of the above should be interpreted to mean that performance measurement doesn't impact budgeting in the real world. It clearly can, and it clearly does. It's just that it doesn't usually impact budgets according to the theory of performance-based budgeting. What performance measures can do is help *you* to get *your* budget passed.

handful of leaders of the performance-based budgeting pack, is a good example of how performance-based budgeting doesn't work in theory (the theory being that budget allocations are being consistently and rationally made on the basis of results) but how it *does* work in something like reality.

First, let's talk about how it doesn't work in theory, and let's take the current biennial budget as Exhibit A. In preparation for pulling together the 1998-1999 budget, the Governor's Office of Budget and Planning sent out a thick book containing very specific instructions to agency heads on how to come up with their basic revenue requests. Now, you're probably expecting to hear that in those instructions, the folks at the GOBP asked agency heads to muster all the performance data they could lay their mitts on and present that data in a way that ties dollars to deeds, past and future, as a way to justify current requests. Well, they did. But then they gave the game away—in the cover letter, actually. "Your request for general revenue-related funds for the 1998-1999 biennium should not exceed the amounts appropriated to your agency for the current biennium," says the letter, signed by the governor, the lieutenant governor and the speaker of the House.

Upon getting this letter, the statesmanlike response of many performance-devoted Texas department heads probably went something like this: *"What? Wait a minute! That's not how performance-based budgeting is supposed to work! What if my performance stinks because I've not been given adequate resources to accomplish the goals of my agency? Or what if I'm achieving incredible things with the little money I have! Just think of what I could do with a 10 percent increase! Plus you said that childhood immunization was going to be a statewide priority in this biennium, and now you're telling me to hold the line on spending when thousands of kids out there need vaccination shots! This is performance-based budgeting? It sounds like a good old-fashioned budget freeze to me!"*

And they were right; that's exactly what it was.

But that's not to say that performance-based budgeting doesn't exist in Texas. It does, and in two forms.

The first is embodied in that thick book of budget-preparation instructions that the governor's budget and planning office sent to all executive and administrative agencies to help guide them in writing their 1998-1999 budget requests. Inside, the book details for agency budgeteers how to tie (in this case, fixed) dollars to priority results. The governor's message here is abundantly clear: Here's the money; set your priorities using performance measurement criteria, then get the job done with the resources you've got. While officially using performance criteria to set those priorities might be new and exciting for some agency directors, the fundamental message of hold the line on spending is certainly not.

But there is another type of performance-based budgeting going on in Texas that ought to be inspirational to all agency heads out there who are competing for tight budget dollars these days: Among the agencies that have fared best budgetarily in Texas are those that have been able to present to the legislature evidence of strong—or improved—performance.

The Texas Department of Insurance, a large regulatory agency with a long-standing reputation for inefficiency, was, early on in the administration of Governor George W. Bush, squarely in the legislature's budget crosshairs. That changed under its new director, Elton Bomer, who in 1995 initiated a sweeping performance-based overhaul of the department. "He was able to go to the legislature and was able to lay out a compelling case for what the department had done and why their budget should not be reduced further," says Ara Merjanian, point man for performance in Governor Bush's office.

In other words, Bomer wasn't about to wander into the budget hearings with the old line-item budget, asking that his biennial allotment merely keep up with inflation. He went in and made his case for salvation based on detailed performance data. (It also didn't hurt that Bomer was a former and well-respected state legislator.)

The moral of all this: When somebody starts talking about the wondrous benefits of performance-based budgeting, you need to think of it not as a new, rational approach to allocating dollars, but rather as a game of covering your fiscal flank by making the case for *your* allocation request as solidly as possible. There is no way that the legislature of any government of any significant size is going to go through every agency, program by program, looking for direct links of dollars to outcomes, all in view of long-range plans and acute public need, and then make a "rational" decision about budgeting—at least not anytime soon. However, that doesn't mean that smart agency and department heads can't go ahead and establish those links for a legislature themselves.

Federal-level officials are also figuring this out. When it comes to budget requests, says Craig Johnstone, at the U.S. State Department, "we tell our people all the time that presumably you're running these programs to achieve specific goals and objectives, so you shouldn't have any qualms about listing those goals and objectives" when budget-hearing time rolls around.

The corollary to the "protect your fiscal flank" imperative of performance-based budgeting is that *not* having measures in place can be fatal. Texas wiped out a $1.5 million program aimed at helping compulsive gamblers because the program couldn't prove it had any impact at all on the relative health and well-being of its immediate customers. Granted, it doesn't sound like a budget line item that would have a very together constituency (after all, they're all busy embezzling money from Granny's estate to cover their escalating losses, rather than writing letters to their local legislator about the need for a smartly run state-funded intervention program). And so the program, in the absence of any proof that it was doing any good at all, went down without so much as an oil slick. (The Texas state lottery, meanwhile, continues to do a booming business.)

But there are documented winners in the performance-based budgeting sweepstakes, and they are worth considering as you face the prospect of performance-based budgeting yourself. One of them is Prince William County Police Chief Charlie Deane, whose story you'll recall from Chapter Two. After taking a public beating about his performance in the whole area of "clearance rates" when compared with nearby counties, Deane got mad. Mad enough to muster his own documentation about clearance rates illustrating that his performance in clearing cases was actually superb considering that his was the most short-staffed department of any county in the area—and that his department was using a particularly stringent definition of what constitutes a "cleared" case: the perp had to be caught, tried and convicted.

The county council, attuned to the persuasive power of performance, was swayed by Deane's data. And so the council agreed to increase his annual manpower allotment, but with one key condition: In return for the fresh troops, Deane is being held to new and higher levels of performance. That's fine with Deane; he's already proved he's up to the challenge.

The Future of Performance-Based Budgeting

How the purer variety of performance-based budgeting plays out in the future will be interesting to watch. Clearly, quite a few state and local governments are getting very good at tying deeds to dollars in internal budget documents. "Certainly in a state like Texas, the architecture is in place," says Wilson Campbell, who used to work in Texas on the performance-based budgeting effort and now is helping the Governmental Accounting Standards Board develop and sell Service Efforts and Accomplishments reporting. And clearly there is growing interest among some legislators in the whole business of performance measurement and performance budgeting, so a number of jurisdictions bear watching.

Among them is the commonwealth of Virginia, where budget officials are being strategic and realistic in their approach to performance-based budgeting. Virginia is easing into performance-based budgeting slowly. It has asked agencies to begin including a limited number of core results indicators into their budgets (rather than go the Oregon or Texas kitchen-sink route), simply to get executive and legislative branch officials comfortable with measures; budget officials in Virginia don't expect that legislators are going to immediately begin devouring performance data like gumdrops. But Herb Hill, state planning and evaluation manager with the Virginia Department of Planning and Budget, says he's seeing progress. He has, for example, noticed that some of the younger legislators do seem interested in decent performance data when it comes budget time. "We're not saying that we expect all budget decisions will ride on recommendations supported by performance data," says Hill, "but they are another piece. Some legislators are getting used to that and some aren't; a lot of it is a matter of education." And Hill's office has come up with some pretty creative ways to forward everybody's education, one in particular that is worth mentioning: The DPB has deemed that all agency requests for budget increases must be accompanied by specific performance data outlining what the increase will buy—not a bad way to get everybody's attention focused on outcomes.

And certainly if GASB decides to make Service Efforts and Accomplishments reporting mandatory, that will also raise the profile of results as one of the more essential ingredients in budgeting.

The bottom line, though, is that anything like textbook performance-based budgeting will continue to be an extreme rarity for the foreseeable future, and for two simple reasons: It's hard to do well, and to the extent that legislators even understand it, they like it in theory, but they aren't so enthusiastic about it in practice.

Chapter 8 Quick Quiz

1. Supporting a "performance management" program in your agency is a good way to:
    a. spend $1,000 a day to learn that you should "think outside the box" (or is it "color outside the box")?.
    b. come up with some new cool-looking flow charts.
    c. finally sink the TQM effort you've been trying to torpedo for the past four years.

2. The reason your legislature supports "performance-based budgeting" is:
    a. it has a nice constituency-pleasing ring to it.
    b. a large, expensive national accounting firm told them they should.
    c. it seems to work for Sillyvale, Sunnyfornia.

3. The chances that the United States Congress will follow through on anything like a performance-based budgeting initiative are:
    a. two billion to one.
    b. two trillion to one.
    c. about the same as a compulsive Texas gambler's chances of entering a state-funded rehab program.

4. A good reason for helping develop solid performance measures for your agency is:
    a. whether or not the legislature ever takes the data seriously at budget time, it could lead to significant internal management improvements.
    b. there's a much better chance that at budget hearing time you'll be able to make your case to the legislature.
    c. the Governmental Accounting Standards Board may soon require you to.
    d. all the above.

CHAPTER NINE

The New Focus on Results; Or How a Pig Named Harley Transformed Intergovernmental Relations (Or Tried to, Anyway)

Performance measurement extended logically could have one other powerful effect on government besides its broad impact on management and potentially broad impact on budgeting: It could shift the focus of government away from its current preoccupation with rules and regulation—process—to results.

Yuck. What a nauseating lead paragraph. It sounds like it came straight out of one of those books on reinventing government. The genre is familiar to you: Every page is loaded with words like "should," "must" and "have to," dead giveaways that the authors are either academics, consultants or former administrators from that previously mentioned mythical California municipality.

The fact of the matter is that rules are always going to be a big part of public administration. Life is just easier when you treat everybody in a public-sector setting in the exact same way regardless of circumstances; that's why rules were invented. When you take judgment out of decision-making, it saves you the headache of being accused of treating different people differently for nefarious reasons (since you will certainly never be accused of doing it for sensible reasons). As a result, everyone gets jumped through the same hoops, whether that makes sense or not and whether you or they like it or not. Besides, most people in government love the certainty embodied in a good restrictive rule, no matter how nonsensical that rule might be given the task at hand; few people like to actually make decisions, especially decisions that might be judged or second-guessed. And, finally, people in positions of authority love the power vested in them in enforcing a good restrictive rule, no matter how nonsensical that rule might be given the task at hand. That's just human nature. Plus, if you have to make a very unpopular decision, it's great to be able to fall back on that good old standby: "Sorry, but those are the rules."

So let's dispense right off the bat with the notion that somehow government is going to ever become so purely results-driven that rules and regulations are going to go away to any significant degree. It's just not going to happen.

However, there are very specific transactions within the enterprise of government where a focus on results is showing some potential (note the words "potential" and "some") to make life a little simpler and clearer—and even happier—for all involved: in government contracts with the private sector, in the regulatory arena and in the area of intergovernmental agreements.

You Do This; I Give You Money

Let's start with contracting. The concept of making payment contingent on some previously agreed-upon level of performance or set of results isn't new (although actually holding a contractor to its side of the bargain might be). Those parts of government involved in building things like highways, school buildings and aircraft carriers have long been in the business of writing performance-based contracts. However, governments are starting to try performance contracting in areas not previously regarded as likely candidates. This is particularly true in the whole area of social services delivery, a program category that is famous for focusing on out*puts*—how many people were run through a particular program—rather than out*comes*—how many of the people coming out of the program were actually drug-free, or ready to be kind to their kids, or possessing skills that might actually allow them to hold a decent job.

A pioneer of the practice is Ramsey County, Minnesota, which started to emphasize performance in its relationship with its social services contractors nearly 20 years ago. The shift was due mostly to the fact that the local press was having a field day with stories about mistreatment of clients and mismanagement of programs, and was happily hammering the county commission with questions about the lousy performance of the county's social service contractors. The commissioners didn't have very many good answers to these questions. And so the county commission made a logical, but at the time radical, decision: It would set up an office of research and evaluation to come up with performance measures—in areas from mental health services, to services for children and adults, to services for the developmentally disabled—in order to start getting some clearer idea of what sorts of service efforts and accomplishments the county was actually buying with taxpayer dollars. This wasn't an easy undertaking. Having no baseline by which to judge performance, it was a start-from-square-one exercise. As it has evolved, the Ramsey County program is not a pure performance-based contracting system. In other words, the county doesn't make reimbursement contingent on some level of previously agreed-upon performance. Rather, the county regularly and systematically reviews the performance of all its social services contractors, an exercise that it finds relatively easy to do today because of a decade and a half of refining its measures and developing baselines for acceptable performance. Contractors that appear to be having problems get special attention—not punitive attention, at first, but help. In fact, a frequent tactic of the county is to put a top-performing contractor together with a poor performer so that the poor performer might learn how to operate more effectively.

A small handful of other jurisdictions, on the other hand, are trying purer forms of performance-based contracting, demanding specific levels of performance as a condition of reimbursement.

One of the purest of these efforts is a pilot program in Oklahoma called the Milestone Payment System, developed by the state's Department of Rehabilitation Services, which is responsible for placing developmentally disabled, physically disabled or mentally ill Oklahomans into jobs. Under the Milestone system, contractors receive 10 percent of their payment for determining a client's needs, 10 percent upon a client's completing vocational training, 10 percent upon job placement, 20 percent once that client has been in the job for a month, and so forth, with full payment being made after a client has been working at the same job for 90 days. To discourage "creaming" of the easiest-to-place clients, the department pays more for clients deemed to be "highly challenged."

One would guess that such a system would not be wildly

popular with contractors. After all, for decades they had been skating along, producing all kinds of numbers on caseloads and caseworker hours, while never actually being asked whether they were helping anybody or not. But rather than rebelling against the new way of doing business, social services contractors—after some initial skepticism—actually seem to like it. The system, contractors say, has freed them up to actually do their job: get clients ready for and into real work. According to one contractor, staffers under the old activities-driven reimbursement system used to spend 20 percent of their day filling out the billable-hours sheets (in 15-minute increments) that the state required for reimbursement. Now they spend that time working with clients to get them work ready and with potential employers who might want to hire them.

It's worth highlighting one of the main reasons why the shift to performance-based contracting went so smoothly in Oklahoma: Contractors were brought in to help develop the system right from the start, which was a smart move by Department of Rehabilitation Services officials for two reasons: It helped defuse suspicion, and it probably led to a more sensible set of performance measures than would have come out of a purely government-configured plan.

Of course, some might dismiss the Oklahoma example as unreplicable in places with bigger caseloads and bigger problems. And so one other effort at tying performance to dollars should be mentioned here, this one in a more difficult setting. In fact, thinking about it, it would be hard to come up with a tougher place or more intractable population than these: New York City and the homeless.

In New York City, the Department of Homeless Services now has a "Performance Incentive Program" that it is using as a way to phase in performance-based contracting. Currently, service providers that perform well can win a bonus of up to 3 percent above their annual contracts. According to DHS Director Gordon Campbell, the bonuses can be used very flexibly. All DHS asks is that the spending have some nexus with the goal of helping the homeless become independent (for example, service providers could use some of the money to offer performance bonuses to their own staff). One of the major criteria used by the department to judge whether a contractor deserves a bonus is percentage of clients placed in permanent housing, using a formula that includes placements, recidivism and overall contractor performance (see "Helping the Homeless by the Numbers" on the next page).

The bonuses are just a start, however. Next year, 15 to 20 percent of each service provider's contract will be performance-based, according to Campbell, who has been working for two years on the new reimbursement system. In developing its performance-based contracts, DHS is also working on formulas that will allow DHS to weight "performance" according to how difficult a population is to serve, an attempt—as they've tried in Oklahoma—to address that age-old worry about creaming in performance contracting.

Among the performance measures that DHS currently tracks:

- Placements in permanent housing.
- Rates of recidivism into any part of the shelter system.
- Rates of school registration and attendance (for families in the system).

Technically, the DHS measures tend toward out*puts* more than out*comes*, but, again, a measure such as "placements in permanent housing" can probably be considered an "interim" or "surrogate" outcome measure on the safe assumption that getting homeless people into permanent housing is an important first step in helping them become independent.

There is one other performance-based social services contract that should be noted. Under welfare reform, the federal government has given states specific targets to achieve in roll reduction and levels of employment (or activity that is employment-related) as a condition of future funding. We'll

Helping the Homeless by the Numbers

The New York City Department of Homeless Services offers its privately run shelters and drop-in centers the chance to win a 3 percent bonus above their annual city contracts. Here, for readers who like nothing more than working up a nice regression equation before breakfast, are a couple of ways that DHS calculates the bonus (for other readers, don't worry; this won't be on the quiz):

Basic Formula: (.50) x [placements into housing] + (.30) x [placements who don't return in 6 months] + (.20) x [overall contract performance] = total score.

Each variable in brackets is based on a goal for the shelter type (General, Employment, Mental Health, Substance Abuse and Transitional). Each provider will receive a score of from 0 to 3 for each variable depending on the amount by which they exceed their goal.

Drop-In Centers Formula: (.1) x [development of service plans] + (.1) x [placement into programs] + (.5) x [placements into housing] + (.3) x [placements who don't return in 6 months] = total score.

Each variable in brackets is based on a goal that will be the same for all providers. Those who meet or exceed the goal will receive credit for that variable.

get more into the particulars of the arrangement later in this chapter. But for the time being, suffice it to say that the current federal welfare law has to be considered the grandaddy of all performance-based social services contracts.

And while we're on the subject of large-scale performance-based contracts, we might as well throw in one other: Currently, the U.S. is balking at anteing up what it owes the United Nations. Why? The short answer that some congressional opponents of the payment give is that there's no proof that the *lack* of payment has had any impact on the *outcome* of individual issues or incidents in which the U.N. has been involved. In fact, Congress commissioned a whole GAO report to support that contention. Which just goes to show you that Congress *will* pay attention to performance measures in making budget decisions...when it is politically convenient to do so.

The New Regulators; Or Mister Rogers Takes Over the EPA

The same sort of focus on the bottom line is also gaining some currency in the regulatory world. Again, nothing is ever going to replace a good old stiff fine and jail sentence, but some federal agencies, such as EPA and OSHA, have for several years now been looking at ways to be less reactive and punitive and more focused on cooperating in the name of results. So rather than confining themselves to dictating solutions to various problems and then knocking heads when regulatees don't perform up to snuff, EPA and OSHA are learning to step back and give businesses at least the initial opportunity to prove they're worthy of being trusted to come up with their own ways to run cleanly and/or safely in consultation with regulators.

As you'll recall from Chapter Four, under the EPA's "33/50" program, back in 1988 regulators asked industry to voluntarily reduce emissions of certain common pollutants by 33 percent by 1992 and by 50 percent by 1995. Freed to decide for themselves how to do that, those companies that were discharging the offending materials hit the targets well before the deadlines set by EPA. And we also learned in Chapter Four what great things OSHA found it could accomplish when it started to really focus on the myriad ways in which Maineiacs were hurting themselves, and what could be done to work with businesses (and employees, not incidentally) to reduce injuries.

This new approach to more targeted, cooperation-based compliance has already proved itself at the state government level. Minnesota, Florida and Kansas have for a few years now been emphasizing customer service and compliance over audits and punishment in their revenue departments. When Minnesota first piloted this in its sales tax operation, the results were immediate and impressive—better compliance and higher collections. The state learned a valuable lesson: It wasn't so much that taxpayers didn't want to cough up the dough, it was that the whole system for collection was so user-unfriendly that many—particularly the little mom-and-pop stores—were simply having a tough time complying. All three states have documented significant increases in compliance rates—and tax receipts—in the wake of this new focus on results; Kansas, for example, reported adding 4,000 taxpayers to the rolls using honey rather than violations. (Incidentally, for one of the most incredibly detailed performance reports you'll see come out of any government office anywhere, write to the Florida Department of Revenue, 104 Carlton Bldg., Tallahassee, FL 32399-0100 and ask for a copy of one of the department's "Monthly Performance Reports.")

And states and localities, alike, are trying to effect a more cooperative posture on cleaning up brownfields. Instead of just trying to affix blame and levy gigantic fines, a number of jurisdictions, from Wichita, Kansas, to the state of Pennsylvania, are now working with business and industry more cooperatively to get old industrial sites cleaned up, rather than spending huge amounts of money and energy fighting over who is liable for the mess.

While "cooperative compliance" rolls off the tongue easily, some words of caution are in order. First, in many regulatory bureaucracies, there remains a cadre of enforcers who are suspicious of all this cooperation business. And for good reason. They've been burned before by businesses that faked right and then went wrong. Having been burned before, those hard-bitten enforcers will be a hard sell. Second, there *is* a danger that regulators may get too close to their "customers," and ease off a bit when the opposite tack—bearing down—might be what's called for. And third, it's naive to believe that a certain percentage of laggards out there won't take every inch of slack they're given and run with it. Which is why any cooperation-based approach to regulation needs to rest on that time-tested maxim of nuclear arms control: "Trust, but verify."

Having said all that, the evidence is solid that a more cooperative regulatory approach—one that really does emphasize results over rules—can be effective. Plus it tends to ease the tension generally between government and citizens and between government and businesses, and that just accrues to the benefit of democracy.

The New, New, Really New, Just-Came-in-Yesterday Federalism

Being busted by a pig must be humiliating enough. But being busted by the feds for busting people with a pig was beyond the pale. And so began the saga of Harley the drug-sniffing Vietnamese pot-bellied pig, who was signed on by the Portland, Oregon, police department in the early 1990s to track down illicit drugs.

Although it was documented that the pig did a better job at drug interdiction than dogs (plus he never growled at anybody) and that he was cheaper to keep (apparently he wasn't tremendously fussy about food), officials at the U.S. Drug Enforcement Administration ruled that federal funds couldn't be used to support the pig because he wasn't a dog, and the federal grant authority language was clear: Federal money could only be used to pay for dogs (although the rules didn't specifically *exclude* pigs, a clear oversight on the part of some slack regulation-writer).

And so Harley was seized upon by Vice President Al Gore as a classic case of nonsensical federal rules getting in the way of government performance. At the time, Gore was up to his kneecaps in reinventing the federal government through his National Performance Review, which he had set up to comb through the federal government to look for inefficiency, duplication and, as in the case of the pig, stupidity.

And it was Harley the pig that the vice president used as his poster child—or poster pig—to argue that it was time to launch a new era of intergovernmental relations, an era when governments work together to shift from a focus on rules to a focus on results.

This wasn't a new idea. As states and localities have become more serious about developing good outcome measures, they have been trying to sell the feds (and each other) on exactly this new type of intergovernmental compact: Cut the rules and regulations, and instead hold us accountable for certain levels of agreed-upon results. If we don't live up to our end of the bargain, then you may step in and abrogate the agreement, seize control of the program, cut our funding, reinstate the rules, fine us, make bacon out of the pig, or whatever.

As mentioned above, that's the basic agreement underpinning the current effort at national welfare reform. The feds have granted states unprecedented freedom in how they administer the mainstay welfare program, Temporary Assistance to Needy Families (the program that replaced Aid to Families With Dependent Children). In return, states are required to meet certain levels of performance. If states don't live up to those performance levels, they get docked a certain amount of federal money. More work is currently being done on the measures that the feds are using to judge state performance—the initial ones being awfully simplistic and too focused on blunt outcomes such as cutting caseloads, which many argue have had the perverse results of inspiring (and rewarding) pure case-dumping. But anecdotally, at least, the new arrangement seems to be allowing states to move toward crafting the type of results-focused and seamless public assistance programs that they've been clamoring after for decades. At the same time, a number of states are passing this newfound flexibility down the governmental food chain, allowing local governments (or state offices working at the local level) to come up with their own custom-crafted and creative solutions for helping people become self-sufficient, too.

In Ohio, for example, the state has handed counties significant flexibility in how they design their overall social services programs, in essence granting people like Montgomery County Social Services Director Steve Rice his longest-standing wish: "Just give me my $400 million and tell me what you want me to accomplish; don't tell me how to accomplish it." (North Carolina is applying this same approach to early childhood health and development on a pure state-to-local level. Through it's "Smart Start" program, the state is allowing counties much more flexibility in how they spend state money in return for a county-wide plan that includes clear performance measures.)

On a much broader front, EPA is currently working with all 50 states to come up with "performance partnership agreements," which, in essence, offer states freedom to mingle program money and duck red tape in return for a commitment to achieve certain levels of environmental cleanup and protection. While there is considerable resistance to this new deal among EPA's enforcement Old Guard—many of whom have never, apparently, met a state environmental official that they trusted—the effort is moving ahead and certainly has tremendous potential for bringing greater efficiency and more common sense to environmental protection, particularly if states hold up their end of the bargain.

And some appear very ready to do that. Florida, for example, has signed a "Joint Compliance and Enforcement Plan" with the EPA that gives the state considerable discretion in how it approaches the whole issue of enforcement and compliance. Underpinning the agreement is the state's Environmental Performance Measurement System, which monitors environmental quality on an "ecosystem" basis. To prove it's doing the job, the Florida Department of Environmental Protection is now producing quarterly reports covering everything from the health of its estuaries to the breathability of its air. (The effort has paid other dividends; in getting more serious about measures, the state has discovered some new and previously unsuspected sources of water pollution that it is now addressing.)

Following EPA's lead, the U.S. Department of Labor and U.S. Department of Education are offering their own versions of regulatory flexibility, called "workflex" and "edflex," respectively. Under workflex and edflex, states are allowed to apply for waivers from the two federal departments in order to sidestep rules and focus programs and program money where the states think they need it most. (The feds have added an interesting twist to the arrangement: In return for such a waiver, states have to agree to remove their own rules and regulations binding local governments under parallel state programs.) Again, this flexibility is granted in return for some agreed-upon level of performance.

Seeking Flexibility in Harley's Home State

A significant pilot for all this flexing has been Oregon, which in 1994 negotiated something of an umbrella waiver with the federal government known as "the Oregon Option."

In essence, the Oregon Option is a memorandum of understanding among the feds and state and local officials that calls on all interested parties to work together on a broad front—from health care to workforce development, education to natural resources—to look to results rather than rules and regulations in coordinating and expediting intergovernmental action. The bottom-line promise of the O.O.: Rules and regulations that get in the way of results ought to go.

At the time it was launched, the Oregon Option was hailed as the bold new frontier of intergovernmental cooperation, and initially it made some interesting and promising progress. For example, in the first year, the intergovernmental group working on child health issues was able to remove a number of administrative barriers to helping streamline the state's ambitious child immunization effort, which state officials argue led to an increase in the state's immunization rate for 2-year-olds of a hefty 70 percent. That same year, the U.S. Department of Health and Human Services agreed to fast-track a waiver request that allowed Oregon to merge several social services funding streams in order to better integrate state and local programs (remember, this was pre-1996 welfare reform). Small steps, but harbingers of good things to come, officials hoped.

But even within those early successes was evidence that this wasn't going to be easy. The request to HHS to allow the state to merge social services funding streams was initially put on the siding with other state waiver requests. Oregon officials—having assumed that the Option meant special treatment for Oregon—were understandably miffed, but didn't really make any progress with HHS officials until Vice President Gore was apprised of the stalemate and enlisted to get the waiver back on the fast track, which he did. But obviously, for the Oregon Option to work, other federal officials besides the vice president of the United States were going to have to get into the spirit of the thing.

It wasn't just federal officials who were reluctant to break out of old patterns of behavior, though. State and local officials in Oregon and special-interest groups, alike, all have pet projects or cherished territory that they have found difficult to give up. Any time you crack a federal pipeline program, some of the cash is going to flow away from the interests that helped create that program; every time you find a way to skirt a rule, somebody's turf has been carved away. So there will always be some institutional resistance to "flexing."

But even if the Oregon Option hasn't always been the red carpet through federal red tape that state and local officials hoped it would be, people are still working at it. On the symbolism front, Vice President Gore changed the name of the National Performance Review to the National Partnership for Reinventing Government. And those on the Oregon Option front lines report pockets of progress. For example, HHS officials seem to have recovered from their early backsliding on that initial waiver request and are getting high marks for at least trying to streamline rules and regulations where laws allow them to. Department of Agriculture officials, on the other hand, are reported to be locked into an intergovernmental cooperation mindset that puts them somewhere in the late 1950s.

It is, of course, unrealistic to expect the Oregon Option to transform intergovernmental relationships in just a few years. And people working at it at the ground level are appropriately philosophical: "I can't say we've achieved dramatic results," says a county official who has been in the middle of trying to make the Oregon Option work across several program areas, "but at least there's an openness to discussion."

And in its small successes—even if that success amounts to little more than state, local and federal officials sitting down around one table and agreeing that everyone in the room is supposed to be working toward a similar goal, whether that goal is to help kids get vaccinated or find families housing—there is that distant glimmer of hope that a focus on results really can change how governments relate to one another.

Which is a good place to end this book. Performance measurement is not magic; it's a lot of work; not everybody gets it, or wants to get it; it's probably politically impossible to even try in some places; and it's not the answer to every problem facing government everywhere. But when applied sensibly and in the right setting, it has the potential to help government do its job better—or at least to allow governments to start asking why certain jobs don't seem to be getting done as well as they should be. And for those governments that do begin to focus on results, there is one other potential benefit: that citizens will begin to understand better the connection between their tax dollars and what government is trying to accomplish.

Chapter 9 Quick Quiz

1. An important criterion when deciding on whether to pay a contractor is:
    a. he is related to you by marriage.
    b. he is related by marriage to the legislator who oversees your program.
    c. the contractor delivered on agreed-upon results.

2. An effective regulatory program focuses on:
    a. an escalating system of hefty fines.
    b. an analysis of violations in relation to lunar cycles.
    c. prevention and cooperation/flexibility and verification.

3. A good way to support an intergovernmental cooperative agreement would be:
    a. not telling anyone else in your office that such an agreement exists.
    b. sending the person in your office with the least authority and seniority to all major meetings of the intergovernmental players.
    c. giving up a little turf and authority while sharing all pertinent information with your intergovernmental partners.

If You're Still Serious...

Congratulations: You're on the verge of actually reading an entire book on public administration all the way through. The only other people to have ever actually read an entire book on public administration all the way through are: (a) the author of the book; (b) his/her editor (maybe); (c) nobody.

In fact, try this at the next (and, incidentally, last) cocktail party you're invited to and see what happens: "Gee, I've just finished an entire and entirely fascinating book on performance measurement in the public sector." You will get something akin to the look that I get whenever I share a bit of local gossip with my next-door neighbor's one-eyed terrier. It's a distant and milky gaze indicating that very little in the way of real communication is taking place. The upshot being that this book will no doubt soon take its rightful place under the dying geranium on your windowsill.

But before you put it there, you're going to need some other books, reports and so forth on performance measurement in order to actually learn something worthwhile on the subject.

While it would be easy to succumb to the temptation to lard up the listing that follows with the title of every book, article, report, primer, vision statement or budget document related to performance measurement that I've collected (and in some cases actually tried to plow through) in the last seven years, I'll resist and keep it short.

In general, there is a ton of good information out there on performance measurement in local government. There is a lot of good information on performance measurement in state government. There is a little bit of good information on performance measurement in the federal government. And then there are a handful of good general primers on the subject.

But the fact is that for anyone at any level of government struggling with any of this, the concepts behind performance measurement are basically all transferable. If you understand the difference between an output measure and an outcome measure, you're halfway there. It's just a matter of adapting those basic concepts to your particular situation. In fact, it wouldn't hurt a federal or state official at all to go ahead and get a copy of *How Effective Are Your Community Services? Procedures for Measuring Their Quality*, which covers performance measurement in local government. Nor would it be inappropriate for a state or local government official to take a look at the U.S. State Department's *Strategic Plan for International Affairs* for an example of how a governmental entity with a fairly amorphous mission has gamely wrestled it down to a more tangible proposition through its strategic plan.

With that in mind, I'd suggest checking out some combination of the following:

How Effective Are Your Community Services? Procedures for Measuring Their Quality, published by the Urban Institute and the International City/County Management Association. Available by calling 800-745-8780; ask for item #40617; individual copies are $55.

This is the bible for any municipal official who is serious about performance measurement, and will save you a lot of wheel-spinning if you get a copy and read it before embarking on a performance measurement program. While aimed at local officials, it is a book that could be of benefit to anybody who is interested in learning the nitty-gritty of performance measurement. Although it gets as specific as how to measure the effectiveness of your fire service and water works, it also offers solid primers on such general topics as handling citizen complaints and rating the quality of services and facilities using "trained observers."

Service Efforts and Accomplishments Reporting: Its Time Has Come; an Overview, published by and available through the Governmental Accounting Standards Board, 401 Merritt 7, P.O. Box 5116, Norwalk, CT 06856-5116. To order, call 203-847-0700, ext. 10. Individual copies are $20.

Readability isn't exactly its hallmark, but it delivers the meat of the matter when it comes to measuring local government performance in everything from law enforcement to public health to road maintenance to public assistance. Along with the book, you'll want to get a copy of GASB's *Concepts Statement No. 2*, related to service efforts and accomplishments reporting.

Reaching Public Goals: Managing Government for Results, published by the National Partnership for Reinventing Government (formerly the National Performance Review) and available by sending $7.50 to the U.S. Government Bookstore, McPherson Square, 1510 H St. N.W., Washington, DC 20005-1008.

It is a compendium of Web sites, publications and contacts at all levels of government, all related to performance measurement. Well worth thumbing through.

Results-Oriented Government: A Guide to Strategic Planning and Performance Measurement in the Public Sector, published by the Southern Growth Policies Board and the Southern Consortium of University Public Service Organizations and available through SGPB at P.O. Box 12293, Research Triangle Park, NC 27709; 919-941-5145.

This booklet has a Dick-and-Jane quality to it that hardened veterans of public administration will find a little hard to take, but it is a concise and well-grounded primer on performance measurement, from strategic planning to sustaining a performance measurement effort. And if you find the booklet valuable, SGPB has developed a full-blown performance measurement study program that goes with it.

Measuring Program Outcomes: A Practical Approach, published by the United Way of America. Copies are $25 (there is a discount for not-for-profit organizations). Call 800-772-0008 and ask for Item #0989.

While the book was written to be applied by those involved in human services agencies, it is a terrific step-by-step primer on developing a performance measurement program that anybody, local to federal, in any program area, would find hands-on useful. It offers detailed explanations for everything from putting together the team that is going to develop your performance measurement effort to creating outcome measures that mean something.

Either or both:
• The Texas *Legislative Appropriations Request for the Biennium Beginning September 1, 1999: Detailed Instructions for Executive and Administrative Agencies.* For a copy, write to the Governor's Office of Budget and Planning at 1100 San Jacinto, Room 4.300, Austin, TX 78701. Or you can access it via the Web at www.lbb.state.tx.us.
• The Virginia *1998-2000 Executive Budget*, available through the state's Department of Planning and Budget, 200 N. Ninth St., Room 418, Richmond, VA 23219. Or you can access is via the Web at www.state.va.us/dpb. (In fact, Virginia has a wealth of material on performance-based budgeting, including a handbook for getting started. For more

information, call the department at 804-786-7455.)

Neither state is doing pure performance-based budgeting, but as discussed in Chapter Eight, it is unlikely that *anybody* will ever be doing pure performance-based budgeting. Both states have, though, put a very solid performance measurement base under their budgets, and both, arguably, are slowly boxing their legislatures into the position of having to at least acknowledge the existence of good data on performance (and, one would hope, occasionally act on it). For other jurisdictions interested in doing that, both of these publication are excellent roadmaps. And while we're on the subject of budgeting, it's probably no coincidence that the two states with performance-budgeting systems that are among the most advanced in the country operate on two-year budget cycles.

Accountability for Performance: Measurement and Monitoring in Local Government, published by the International City/County Management Association and available by calling 800-745-8780; ask for item #42016; individual copies are $23.95.

A more general but very solid primer on performance measurement in local government, with an excellent section—the last chapter in Part I of the book—on activity-based costing. It's probably not a book that everybody needs to read, but if you're being tapped to play a significant role in a performance measurement program—regardless of the level of government in which you're serving—it's worth a look.

Managerial Cost Accounting Concepts and Standards for the Federal Government: Statement of Recommended Accounting Standards Number 4, published by the Federal Accounting Standards Advisory Board and available through the Government Printing Office for $7.50. Call 202-512-1800 and ask for document #04100100457-2, or access it via FASAB's Web site: Go to www.financenet.gov/fasab.htm and click on "standards and concepts." (If none of those work, call FASAB at 202-512-7350.)

If a strong cost accounting component is not part of your overall performance measurement plan, then you need to go back to the chalkboard. None of this makes any sense to do if you can't account for costs in the calculation of performance, and *Number 4* is a first-rate primer on how to connect the two.

Measuring Performance; Strengths and Weaknesses of Research Indicators, published by the U.S. General Accounting Office. Single copies are free. Orders may be placed by phone at 202-512-6000 or by fax at 202-512-2537. Ask for report GAO/RCED-97-91.

Esoteric stuff for those who can't get enough of this, but it is a solid discussion of the difficulties of measuring "results" when the "activity" is research.

Measuring Progress of Estuary Programs; Highlights, published by the U.S. Environmental Protection Agency and available through the EPA's Office of Water, EPA, Washington, DC 20460. Request document #EPA842-B94-009, published in November 1994.

An excellent little case study on measuring the impact of efforts to clean up two estuaries on the East Coast.

Prince William County Budget and *Citizen Satisfaction Survey.* Go to the county's Web site at www.pwcgov.org; both documents are available online. If you must have paper, a limited number of copies of the latest budget and citizen satisfaction survey is available by calling 703-792-6720.

Both documents are first-rate, and, again, good illustrations of how detailed and thorough some jurisdictions have become in trying to measure what they do.

Commercial Motor Carriers: DOT Is Shifting to Performance-Based Standards to Assess Whether Carriers Operate Safely. U.S. General Accounting Office, document number

GAO/RCED-98-8. Single copies are free. Orders may be placed by phone: 202-512-6000; or by fax: 202-512-2537.

A good case study on an agency that is starting to refocus its regulatory function on outcomes rather than outputs. The GAO has quite a few other reports related to federal performance measurement efforts. They can be tracked down on the GAO's Web site at www.gao.gov.

U.S. Department of State Strategic Plan for International Affairs. It's up on the State Department's Web page: www.state.gov.

This is the ultimate argument for why nobody should be exempt from having to measure their performance. The strategic plan offers specific goals and specific indicators in an area—international relations—that most believe defies measurement utterly.

City of Portland Service Efforts and Accomplishments: 1996-97; Seventh Annual Report on City Government Performance, published by the City of Portland, Oregon, Office of the Auditor, available by sending a check for $10 to the Audit Services Division, City of Portland, 1221 S.W. 4th Ave., Room 310, Portland, OR 97204, or download it from the division's Web page at www.ci.portland.or.us/auditor/pdxaudit.htm.

Not only does Portland look at its own performance in the report, it compares itself with six other municipalities in a dozen key areas of performance (cost of water, number of fires, crime rates and so forth). Portland's is without a doubt one of the most intelligently compiled and user-friendly SEA reports currently being published.

Case Studies

American Society for Public Administration Task Force on Government Accomplishment and Accountability (1120 G St. N.W., Suite 700, Washington, DC 20005-3885; 202-393-7878; fax: 202-638-4952; e-mail: dcaspa@aol.com). The Task Force has published a whole—and very worthwhile—

series of case studies in performance measurement in local, state and federal government. A list of those case studies is available by calling the number above. Among those worth checking out are:

• *Use of Strategic Planning and Reinvention and the Implementation of the GPRA, Denver Service Center, National Park Service,* which illustrates how complicated implementing performance measurement can be—particularly in an organization with varied reporting responsibilities and hierarchical relationships—as it follows the Service Center's effort from start to finish.

• *The Development of Performance Measures for Virginia Financial Management and Oversight,* a very sophisticated discussion of implementing performance-based budgeting in the real world.

• *Development and Use of Outcome Information: Portland, Oregon,* a really good treatise on lessons learned, written by one of the most seasoned veterans in the performance measurement world, Dick Tracy, the director of audits for the city.

Other Resources

• The Oregon Progress Board has a Web site with links to lots of other performance measurement sites (including federal government sites): www.econ.state.or.us/opb.

• The Iowa Department of Management's Web site is also worth a look, at www.state.ia.us/government/dom/index.html. Good material on activity-based costing is being added every day. You can download the department's ABC Handbook.

• The International City/County Management Association has established a Center for Performance Measurement, which offers extensive technical assistance, contacts with other jurisdictions involved in performance measurement, and even computer software to help get you up and measuring. Contact the ICMA Center for Performance Measurement at 777 N. Capitol St. N.E., Suite 500, Washington, DC 20002-4201; 202-962-3589. It is also worth getting a copy of the center's annual *Comparative Performance Measurement* report, the latest of which is for fiscal year 1996. In it you'll find comparisons of the performance of local jurisdictions in areas from the fire service to libraries. Single copies are $50. To order, call 800-745-8780 and ask for publication item #42331.

•The Governmental Accounting Standards Board's Web site is evolving into the best one-stop source of information anywhere on applying performance measures to what government does. Check it out at www.gasb.org.

•The Kennedy School of Government's Visions of Governance in the 21st Century research program will be focusing on, among other things, performance measurement in government. For information, go to www.ksg.harvard.edu/visions/.

Index